D0253376

MVFOL

101 More Drama Games
for Children

Other SmartFun Books

101 Music Games for Children by Jerry Storms

101 More Music Games for Children by Jerry Storms

101 Drama Games for Children by Paul Rooyackers

101 Dance Games for Children by Paul Rooyackers

101 Movement Games for Children by Huberta Wiertsema

101 Language Games for Children by Paul Rooyackers

Coming Soon:

101 More Dance Games for Children by Paul Rooyackers

Yoga Games for Children by Danielle Bersma and Marjoke Visscher

Ordering

Trade bookstores in the U.S. and Canada, please contact:

Publishers Group West
1700 Fourth Street, Berkeley CA 94710
Phone: (800) 788-3123   Fax: (510) 528-3444

Hunter House books are available at bulk discounts for course adoptions;
to qualifying community, health-care, and government organizations;
and for special promotions and fund-raising. For details please contact:

Special Sales Department
Hunter House Inc., PO Box 2914, Alameda CA 94501-0914
Phone: (510) 865-5282   Fax: (510) 865-4295
E-mail: ordering@hunterhouse.com

Individuals can order our books from most bookstores,
by calling toll-free **(800) 266-5592**, or from our
website at **www.hunterhouse.com**

1o1 More Drama Games

FOR

Children

New Fun and Learning with Acting and Make-Believe

Paul Rooyackers

Translated by Amina Marix Evans &
Illustrated by Margreet Hofland

a Hunter House SmartFun book

Library of Congress Cataloging-in-Publication Data
Rooyackers, Paul.
    [Honderd nieuwe dramaspelen. English]
    101 more drama games for children : new fun and learning with acting
and make-believe / Paul Rooyackers ; translated by Amina Marix Evans.— 1st ed.
        p. cm. — (A Hunter House smartfun book)
    Includes index.
    ISBN 0-89793-367-2 (pb) — ISBN 0-89793-368-0 (sp)
    1. Games. 2. Drama. I. Title: One hundred one more drama games for
children. II. Title: One hundred and one more drama games for children. III. Title.
IV. Series.
GV1203 .R58813 2002
793—dc21

           2002027498

Project Credits

Cover Design and Book Production:
  Jil Weil

Book Design: Hunter House

Developmental & Copy Editor:
  Ashley Chase

Proofreader: John David Marion

Acquisitions Editor: Jeanne Brondino

Editor: Alexandra Mummery

Editorial & Production Intern: Claire
  Reilly-Shapiro

Publicity Coordinator:
  Earlita K. Chenault

Sales & Marketing Coordinator:
  JoAnne Retzlaff

Customer Service Manager:
  Christina Sverdrup

Order Fulfillment: Lakdhon Lama

Administrator: Theresa Nelson

Computer Support: Peter Eichelberger

Publisher: Kiran S. Rana

Printed and Bound by Bang Printing, Brainerd, Minnesota

Manufactured in the United States of America
9 8 7 6 5 4 3 2 1   First Edition   02 03 04 05 06

Contents

A detailed list of the games indicating
appropriate age groups begins on the next page.

List of Games

	K– grade 2	Grades 3–5	Grades 6–8	Grades 9–12	All ages
Page · **Game**					
Introduction Games					
9 Flattery Will Get You Everywhere	•	•			
10 In the Hot Seat					•
11 Ready, Set, Alphabet!		•	•		
12 In Character					•
13 Everything Has a Story					•
14 Follow the Feeling	•	•			
15 Worth 1,000 Words			•	•	
16 Alice the Amiable Anteater		•	•	•	
17 Associations					•
18 Solve the Problem!		•	•	•	
Improvisation Games					
20 I Want You to Give Me...		•	•	•	
21 The Storyteller and the Actor		•	•	•	
21 The Gift	•	•			
22 Exchange It	•	•			
23 Spoil the Picture		•	•	•	
24 From Bad to Worse		•	•	•	
25 My Life as a Football		•	•	•	
26 Taking Over			•	•	
27 The Doorbell		•	•	•	
28 Slow Motion		•	•	•	
29 The Interview				•	
Morphing Games					
32 Sport Changes					•
33 The Route		•	•	•	

List of Games, continued

List of Games, continued

List of Games, continued

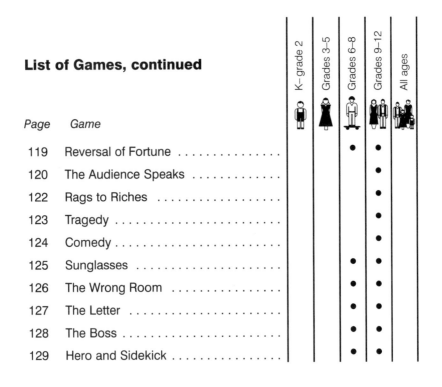

Preface

Our language shows how child's play and drama are intimately connected. We call dramatic works *plays,* and we say an actor *plays* a character on stage. Play is an excellent way for kids to approach drama: Thinking of drama as a game helps them access their native talents for imagination, pretending, and spontaneous fun.

This book contains one hundred and one new drama games. It is both a sequel to and a further development of the original book, *101 Drama Games for Children.* Like the original, this book includes many exercises to develop basic dramatic skills, such as simple mimes, movement exercises, and introduction games. However, this book builds on the first book and places a greater emphasis on performance. This book gives players more opportunities to act out scenes, write scripts, and develop performance pieces. Many of the games will result in works ready for performance at a parents' night or other event. In this book you will also find a greater number of games that are specifically designed for teenagers in junior high and high school. Together, the two books offer a wealth of possibilities for planning play sessions with an ever-increasing number of variations.

These drama games are ideally suited for drama classes in a school, camp, or workshop setting. They are also useful for public speaking, language arts, ESL, and dance classes. They can be used as warm-ups for a group rehearsing a play together or as activities for camp and after-school groups. Many of the games could be adapted for use in creative therapy.

The games have been created and developed in a classroom setting. They are described in detail, so that you can lead them without a great deal of experience in drama or game direction. Still, practice the activities yourself before using them with a group.

Good luck!

Paul Rooyackers
The Netherlands

For easy reading, we have alternated use of the male and female pronouns. Of course, every "he" also means "she," and vice versa!

Introduction

Objectives of the Drama Games

The drama games serve various educational goals applicable to drama, language arts, public speaking, English, and ESL classes. They are also valuable to players' personal and social development. The games are designed to

- **foster creativity**
  The drama games constantly encourage players to stretch their powers of creativity. Ironically, most of us have to learn to be spontaneous: It takes practice to feel comfortable enough on stage to improvise freely. Many of the games require players to take a scene in unexpected directions, exploring possibilities they might not have considered otherwise. The drama games also provide dozens of opportunities for players to make up and develop their own sketches, dialogs, and plays.

- **develop performance skills**
  The games help players become better actors. Players practice improvising as well as acting from a script. They have opportunities to portray a wide variety of characters in situations ranging from ordinary to absurd. They learn to use their voices, expressions, and body language to express different emotions. They also practice using their imaginations to craft a convincing performance.

- **develop language skills**
  Drama games help players become better speakers and

writers. In some games, players write and perform dialogs, dramatic scenes, and plays. In others, they improvise dialogs and skits. The games give players multiple chances to speak in front of an audience, developing their diction, expression, and fluency. Scriptwriting is the perfect medium for reluctant writers. Since the objective is to reproduce the way people talk, perfect grammar is not an issue for scriptwriters. Students may find writing scripts a refreshing change from writing reports, essays, and stories.

- **improve listening and observation skills**
  There is a whole section of observation games designed to help players notice and imitate what they see around them. Even more importantly, players act as the audience for each other. As others perform, players practice listening with respect and reacting honestly but constructively.

- **build social skills: cooperation, trust, respect**
  The games in this book give players ample opportunities to work in pairs, small groups, and as a class. They collaborate on performance pieces: Together they improvise; make up plots; write scripts; make decisions about staging, casting, and so on; and perform in front of an audience. In addition, the book includes a series of trust games to help players develop mutual faith and respect.

- **build self-confidence**
  These drama games let players perform in a noncompetitive setting where there are no stars: Everyone has a chance to shine. Players learn how to express themselves in a group and how others react to them. Practicing self-expression in a fun, low-pressure context helps players overcome shyness and stage fright.

Information for the Leader

The Leader's Role

The leader plays many important roles in conducting these drama games: organizer, director, stage manager, master of ceremonies, cheerleader, and more. Here are a few tips for leading the games. *101 Drama Games* provides even more suggestions. As leader, be sure to

- **think about how players should form pairs or teams.** Players will often want to form teams only with their friends and exclude others. If players consistently play in friendship groups, they will miss opportunities to experience different play styles, and the group will not advance as it should. In order to prevent this, constantly create new ways of forming teams to play the games. Some of the introduction games are specifically designed to produce arbitrary groupings of players. You might also make groups based on similarities such as players' birth months, the initial letters of their names, or the colors of their clothes. Perhaps the simplest way of forming arbitrary teams is to have players count off. For example, to form four teams, have players stand in a line and take turns calling out numbers in sequence from one to four. The number ones form a team, the number twos form another, and so on.

- **agree on signals for directing play.** You may need to give a signal to begin a game or perhaps to interrupt the game so another player can enter. At a group's first meeting, demonstrate a few simple signals to the group and explain what they mean. You might create signals for starting and stopping play, for winding up a game, or for increasing concentration.

- **make it quite clear when the students should take the initiative and when they should follow your guidelines.** Some games involve guided improvisations, while others give players free reign. Let players know whether they should expect direction from you as the game goes on.

- **teach the participants to listen to you and to each other.** Listening and allowing others to finish what they are saying aids not only the progress of the game but the enjoyment as well. Never begin a game until it is quiet and you have sufficient concentration to explain the game properly. Players should not make remarks when someone else is acting, nor should they walk away or otherwise disturb the action. You should be very firm about this because the concentration of the participants is one of the most important elements for staying in character.

- **allow criticism—but only *constructive* criticism.** Teach players how to ask questions about other players' performances. Limiting players to questions rather than comments should help keep the discussion positive. Intervene immediately if you see that someone is planning to make a negative comment.

- **finish each drama game with a short period of time dedicated to reflective silence or some other clear conclusion.** You might end games with a discussion.

How to Combine Games to Form a Comprehensive Program

Each of the drama games can stand alone. The drama games may also be used as the core of a drama program. In the latter case, you can give each class session a logical structure by choosing games to serve various functions. The games are grouped according to type, and each section begins with a brief introduction about the type of game covered. Different types of games can be combined for a play session.

The following types of game are included:

- introduction games
- improvisation games
- morphing games
- observation games
- trust games
- energy games
- situation games
- dialog games
- writing games
- living video games
- game projects
- status games

Athletes first warm up, then play a game, and end with a debriefing. You can give your classes a similar structure. A class lasting an hour requires an introduction of 5–10 minutes, a main activity of 30–40 minutes, and a further 10–15 minutes for finishing up (debriefing and discussion).

Warming Up

The session should always start with a warm-up: a short game to create the right atmosphere. The players will likely enter the room with their minds on other concerns; they need to divest themselves of all distractions in order to concentrate fully on the drama games. You will need to bring the group into the right frame of mind. This can be done using introduction games (see page 8), improvisation games (see page 19), or trust games (see page 52).

The Core

At this point, the group tackles the main activity you have chosen for the players. They might improvise a scene, develop a sketch, or write a script. The purpose of the session now becomes clear. As leader, set yourself a goal that can be worked out during this phase. What do you want to teach the players?

Cooling Down

The participants will leave a session with a wealth of impressions and experiences. They may well be excited by what happened, or perhaps something touched them deeply. A session should always be finished up with a calm moment. Choose a suitable game for this cooling down: perhaps a silent game or a mime exercise. Observation games (see page 41), trust games (see page 52), and energy games (see page 59) are all well suited to the cool-down period. Alternatively, you might use the cool-down period for an evaluation (see below).

The Evaluation

It is very important for the players that you discuss the exercises and performances carefully with them. Be constructive and inspiring in your criticism. Comment on positive aspects that the players can build on personally and as a group. Players need to feel they are in a process of development that you are carefully guiding.

You might want to leave a notebook in the room where players can write down questions or comments. That way, players can give you feedback even if time does not allow for a group discussion or if they have comments they feel uncomfortable making in front of the others.

Key to the Icons Used in the Games

To help you find games suitable for a particular situation, all the games are coded with symbols or icons. These icons tell you at a glance some things about the game:

- the appropriate grade level/age group
- the amount of time needed
- the organization of the players
- the props required
- the space required

These are explained in more detail below.

Suitability in terms of age The age groups correspond to grade level divisions commonly used in the educational system:

= Young children in kindergarten through grade 2 (ages 4 through 8)

= Older children in grades 3 through 5 (ages 8 through 11)

= Adolescents in middle school, grades 6 through 8 (ages 11 through 14)

= Teenagers in high school, grades 9 through 12 (ages 14 through 18)

= All ages

How long the game takes The games are divided into those that require about 5 minutes, 10 minutes, 15 minutes, 30 minutes, 40 minutes or more, and those that require multiple class sessions.

5 minutes   10 minutes   15 minutes

30 minutes   40 minutes or more   multiple sessions

The organization of players All of the games can be adapted to virtually any size of group. The grouping icons indicate how players will be organized to play the game: in pairs, in small groups, as individuals, or all together as a group.

pairs = Players will work in pairs.

small groups = Players will work in small groups.

on your own = Players will work as individuals.

whole group = All the players will work together as a group.

Amount of space needed An ordinary classroom is suitable for most drama games, but now and then a special space (for example, an auditorium) would be even better. Too much decoration is distracting—all the games are best played in an empty space. The games that require a large, gymnasium-sized space are marked with the following icon.

 = Large space needed

Whether you need props Most of the games require no special materials. In some cases props, scenery, audiovisual equipment, or other materials will enhance the game. These games are flagged with the following icon, and the necessary materials are listed under the Props heading.

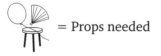 = Props needed

Introduction Games

Introduction games are the perfect way to start a series of classes and bring a new group together. Use these games to introduce your style of working with children and to clearly establish your general ground rules. These games are mental and physical warm-ups, but they are also something more.

Introduction games help people feel at home. Acting is a form of creative expression, and people often feel vulnerable when they express themselves in front of a group. It is important to establish an atmosphere of familiarity and trust. The introduction games set the scene for the later drama games by helping players learn what to expect from each other and how to become comfortable in the group.

An introduction game helps the players get to know each other, but it can also be a personal journey of discovery for each player. Introduction games help players focus on observing and reacting to others, and expressing themselves in front of the group. Players can also learn how others express themselves and how to react to them. These games help players learn to be more comfortable with and knowledgable about themselves in relation to others.

whole group

Flattery Will Get You Everywhere

Have the group stand in a big circle. Call out your own name, then have players call out their names one by one, going counter-clockwise around the circle. Ask players to listen carefully for all the names, and especially the name of the person who comes after them. Go around the circle again, but now have each player call out the name of the neighbor on his right. This way, everyone hears each name twice.

Now look at the player on your right and pay her a compliment, addressing her by name. ("You have a nice, clear speaking voice, Marisa.") Marisa takes her turn, addressing a compliment to the player on her right. ("I love those red pants, Liam.") That person now does the same until everyone has had a turn. You might mix up the circle and play the game again.

2

whole group

In the Hot Seat

Props: a chair (preferably a special one—perhaps a prop throne if you have one on hand)

Place a chair in the center of the room. Sit in the chair and tell players something interesting about yourself—mention a favorite food or hobby, share a secret ambition, describe a place you'd like to visit, say whatever comes to mind. You may want to repeat this preliminary step once in each of the first few class sessions. This way you can help players get to know you better.

Now call on players to sit in the hot seat one by one. Ask players questions about their favorite foods, hobbies, and so on—or invite them to share anything they want. The other players can also ask questions once they are familiar with the game.

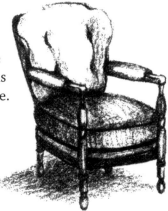

Ready, Set, Alphabet!

Props: alphabet chart (store-bought or handwritten)

Challenge players to arrange themselves in an alphabetical line, according to their first names. Display the alphabet chart if players need to use it for reference. If players don't know each others' names well, they will have to talk amongst themselves to find out whose name starts with *a, b,* and so on. You might suggest areas for players with names at the beginning, middle, or end of the alphabet to gather. If necessary, help players with the details of alphabetization (Adam goes in front of Adele).

Once players are in their line, encourage them to remember their positions. Now ask players to run away from the line and spread out around the room. Signal for them to get back in the line again. Next, ask players to spread out around the room in a different way (hopping, skipping, dragging one leg). Now call out the name of a player—Masako, for instance. That player stands at the head of a new line. The others have to complete the alphabet behind her and when they reach *z,* begin again with *a.* Repeat the game with a new style of moving around the room and have a new player head the line.

In
Character

Have players spread out around the room. Assign a generic character role for everyone in the room to play—a secret agent, a baby, a star athlete, a king, a karate expert.

Tell players that they should move silently around the room, acting out the characteristics and mannerisms of that character. When players approach each other, they should greet each other (silently) in character. Choose a new character and play the game again.

Variations:

- Allow players to speak suitable lines as they act out their characters.

- Assign different roles to all of the players in secret (i.e., whisper the roles in the children's ears or write the roles on cards to be picked out of a hat). Have the players approach and greet one another in character. After a few minutes, ask the players to guess the roles that were acted out by the different children.

Everything Has a Story

Have the group sit in a circle. Explain that you will call out the name of an everyday object—hammer, pillow, sink, pencil, garden hose, or whatever comes to mind—and the player next to you should tell something he has done with that object. For example, the group might hear where the hammer is kept at that player's house or how that player used a hammer to help build a bookcase. When the first player has said his sentence, he calls out a new object for the person next to him. This way everyone gets to know something about the others in the group.

Variation: Players must tell about a problem (real or fictional) they have had with the object mentioned. For example: "I dropped my pencil and it rolled into the storm drain, so I couldn't get it out to write my book report."

Follow
the Feeling

Split up the group into teams of about four players. Choose one player from each group to begin the game as the leader; the rest will be followers. Have each team begin at one side of the room and move to the other side. The leader chooses an emotion and silently moves in a way that shows that feeling. The others follow and imitate the leader. Teams might skulk guiltily, creep suspiciously, or skip exuberantly.

When a team reaches the other side of the room, it chooses another player to lead the team across the room again. Afterwards, you might have teams discuss the emotions they were enacting: Did everyone guess what emotion the leader chose?

Variation: Have the leader create an appropriate sound for the followers to imitate as they move.

Worth 1,000 Words

Props: old photo of each player

In advance, ask players to bring (replaceable) photos that were taken of themselves when they were little. Encourage them to bring snapshots of themselves engaged in an interesting activity, rather than posed portraits.

In the first session, have players sit in a circle with their photos. Ask each player to display his photo and explain what is happening or how he felt at that particular moment. Pass the photo around the circle. The explanations should be no longer than one minute each. Ask players to leave the photos with you until the next session.

In the second session, have players use the photos to make up dramatic situations. In advance, choose a few photos that you feel have the most dramatic potential. Return these photos to their owners. Then divide the group into teams of four to six players, making sure each team includes one player with a photo. Have each team act out the situation in the photo, as explained by the photo's owner. Help teams make sure everyone has a role in the scene: Suggest supporting roles (narrator and so on) if necessary.

Example: The photo might show a player at the age of 2, holding an ice cream cone and sobbing. The scene might include a kid, parents, an ice cream vendor, and so on. Perhaps the kid orders the wrong flavor of ice cream by accident and throws a fit. Will the parents buy a new cone?

Alice the Amiable Anteater

Putting together teams for a new game is often problematic. Friends may want to be together, and to exclude others. This game offers a fun way to form arbitrary groups and get them working together. Divide the alphabet into five or six sections, depending on the number of players. Have all the players whose names begin with the letters *a* through *d* gather together. First initials *e* through *h* should do the same, and so on. Split up or combine teams that are too large or small.

Now have each team make up a short play of about one minute. Each player should use mostly words that begin with her first initial—for example, Anton might play an ape who is an acrobat and loves eating apples, while his teammate Carmela might play a cranky crocodile who chews on carrots.

Have each team present its play in which each team member will play his letter-oriented role.

Associations

Like game 8 (Alice the Amiable Anteater), this game is a fun way to form teams. Ask everyone to sit in a circle. Point out that some words seem to go together: *bread* and *butter*, *eyes* and *see*, *swim* and *water*. Explain that you are going to play a word association game. Tell the group that you will tap one player on the head, and that player should call out a word. Other players should raise their hands if they can think of words that go together with the first word.

Now have players close their eyes and begin. For each player who calls out a word, call on two to four players who raise their hands. These players say their words, leave the circle, and form a team. When all the teams have formed, ask each team to make up a short play using the words they chose.

Example: The first person said *banana skin*; then came the words *slip*, *fall*, and *pain*. The team makes up a sketch using these words.

Solve the Problem!

Props: assignment cards (see description below)

In advance, write a number of dramatic assignments on note cards. Each assignment should involve a problem of some sort. For example:

- Waiting in line to buy a ticket at the station, you realize that your wallet is missing.

- You do the grocery shopping and decide to buy a few extra things. Your mother is not pleased because she had planned to use the money for something else.

- The book you have to take back to the library is damaged. You didn't do it! Who did?

Have one player begin the game by picking an assignment card and then choosing another player to help act out the scene. After a couple of minutes, stop the pair on stage. Ask the first player to sit down and have a new player join the one remaining on stage. Have the new player pick a new assignment card to incorporate into the scene. Repeat this every few minutes.

Improvisation Games

Improvisation blurs the line between acting and playing until the two become one. Isn't a child who is cooking and eating an invisible feast acting? Isn't an actor who is improvising a scene in which aliens land and explore the local mall playing?

Improvisation games can be free or directed. You can give information in advance, as long as it's not too much for players to remember. You can also give players instructions as a game progresses. Some of the assignments described in this section have a specific goal, while others require players to stretch their imaginations. In these games, players must react quickly and think on their feet.

Improvisation games use children's sense of fun to develop skill in acting. They are one of the most important types of drama games.

I Want You to Give Me...

Ask everyone to stand in a big circle. Choose one player to be "It." "It" begins the game by calling out another player's name and saying, "I want you to give me . . . a suitcase." The other player mimes (in a nicely exaggerated way) handing a suitcase to "It." "It" decides what to ask for next. She must mime carrying each item she asks for throughout the game. Of course, a clever player can put all kinds of objects into a suitcase or other packages, but as many as possible of the "given" items should be "visible" to the audience.

Players should use only mime to represent each item: No talking is allowed apart from "It's" requests. If necessary, "It" can speak a few lines and she may be permitted to refuse to carry certain things—or a fixed number of items.

Variation: You could begin a follow-up game by having another player jump in and remark on how heavy all that baggage must be. Then the players can improvise a spoken dialog.

The **Storyteller** and the **Actor**

Have the group sit in a circle. For the first round, take the role of narrator yourself. Choose a volunteer "actor" to act out your story. As you tell your story, the actor should illustrate it using mime and no dialog. Now have two new players act as actor and storyteller.

Variation: Practiced players can make the game humorous or difficult for the actor by getting him to act out all kinds of difficult actions that are almost impossible to mime or totally ridiculous. By doing this, the players create a type of theater of the absurd.

13

The **Gift**

Have everyone sit in a circle. Begin the game by miming that you are holding a wrapped box containing a present. Pass the imaginary present to the player next to you, without saying what it is. The player who receives the present mimes unwrapping it and then uses mime to show the others what it is. Now that player pretends to hold a new wrapped present and passes it to the next player. Keep going until everyone has had a turn.

Exchange It

Have everyone sit in a circle. Mime holding a wrapped present and tell players what it is. Now pass the imaginary package to one of the players. This player "unwraps" it and uses mime to make it very clear that the present is, for instance, a vacuum cleaner. Encourage the player to show whether she likes the present or not. If she does not like the present, she can pass it on to someone who *will* be pleased with it and who enjoys doing the actions that go together with the object. Then it's that person's turn to pass a new a present to another player.

Variation: Something is wrong with the gift: perhaps it is broken or the wrong size. Players should use their actions to show what's wrong, without speaking.

small groups

Spoil the Picture

When something goes wrong in a photo, it can be much more interesting (and certainly funnier) than a perfect picture. For example, a wedding party is posing for its formal portrait in the park. Just as the photographer snaps the picture, a frisbee flies in front of the group and a dog dives to catch it.

Divide the group into teams of about five players each. Each team thinks of a situation where a photographer can take a good photo. When the team is posed, a player from another team (chosen by the leader in advance of the posing) jumps up and joins them, portraying someone who absolutely doesn't belong in such a group. Click: photo!

If this were to happen in real life, the people being photographed would likely become angry, so encourage the players to act out these emotions using gestures that become "frozen" as the imaginary "photo" is taken.

From Bad to Worse

Have players spread out around the room. Explain that you will mention different situations and ask players to act them out. As they act, you will slowly count to ten. Players' actions should get more intense as you count. The situation reaches its climax at ten.

Assignment 1: You are waiting for the bus and you get an itch. It's not bad at first, but it gets worse and worse. You try to hide it as much as you can until that becomes impossible.

Assignment 2: You are standing on the bus and you notice an unpleasant smell. You can't tell where it is coming from, but it's getting stronger.

Assignment 3: The floor starts to get warmer and warmer under your feet. You feel more and more uncomfortable but you don't want to let it show.

Variation: Invite players to think up situations that get more and more intense. Players can take on the role of leader, describing new situations and counting while others act them out.

My Life as a Football

This short game is ideal for quickly warming up or concluding a session.

Have players sit in a circle. Invite them to imagine they are objects—everyday objects, unusual objects, whatever comes to mind. One by one, they stand up to perform a monologue. Each player tells about (and acts out) his experiences as a football, a hurricane, a drinking straw, a watch, and so on. This is an exercise in imagination and it is often very amusing to hear what people think up.

You might prompt players with a simple first sentence, such as, "This morning I was picked up and I knew immediately there was something wrong...."

Variation: Invite players to jump in and take over the story (in the role of the object they have chosen) when they hear a description of an action with which they feel connected. One player may be telling a story as a stapler, and another may take over, transforming the stapler into a watermelon. Players may solve a tricky situation or confuse things even further. The only rule is that the players do not negate each other. A player cannot deny something the other player has just said.

Example:

Player 1: "She stood at the foul line, stared at the basket, and then threw me up in the air...."

Player 2: "And getting thrown up in the air is pretty stressful for a blown-glass paperweight. For a moment I hoped that I'd never come down again...."

Taking Over

Props: a sofa or a few chairs (optional)

This game is good for finishing up a drama session. If there's enough time everyone can act out a quick situation, which can be taken over quickly by other people.

Explain that pairs of players will act out scenes. Other players should watch carefully: When a player has an idea for a different scene that could begin from the position of one of the players on stage, she should clap her hands and take over. When they hear a clap, both players on stage should freeze. The new player will replace one of the players on stage, and start a new scene.

Example: The first pair of players acts out a scene as customer and sales clerk. When the sales clerk starts ringing up the sale on the cash register, another player claps. The players on stage freeze. The new player takes over the sales clerk's position and starts a new scene as a worker typing on a computer. The customer now becomes a worker, too, and joins the new scene. Encourage new players to take over the game every 30 to 60 seconds. As often as possible, have each new player take over the position of the player who has been in the game longest. (In the example above, the next player should ideally replace the player who was the customer in the first scene, rather than the one who started the office worker scene.)

The
Doorbell

Invite a pair of players to act out a short scene. Player A is ringing the doorbell, and player B answers the door. Before the scene starts, have the group decide who player A will be: a cable repair person? the boy next door who kicked his ball into your garden? the woman across the road who's looking for her cat?

Player A makes it clear who it is he has come to see: Is it a 6-year-old child, the ghoulish owner of a haunted house, or the highly respected town mayor? Player B immediately has to take on the role assigned to her. After a minute or two, have another pair start a new scene. Stop each scene before it goes on too long: Encourage partners to bring their scene to a quick climax.

Slow Motion

This game helps players develop their listening and concentration skills. Choose one player to be "It" and have her stand at one end of a large room, facing the wall. Ask the other players to stand at the other end of the room.

Ask "It" to tell a familiar story—a fairy tale, a story read in class, or the plot of a popular movie. As "It" tells the story, the others should mime the story behind her, moving in slow motion. The object of the game is for one of the other players to tag "It" from behind. They can move forward as they mime, but they must limit their motions to what they hear in the story. Watch players and call out any who stop miming or who move too quickly.

As the other players approach, "It" can suddenly stop the story and turn around. When the story stops, players must freeze. Anyone who moves or loses his balance is out. Whoever tags "It" first could start a new game as "It."

Variation: Have the player who is "It" enlist the help of other players in telling the story. Periodically, she calls out the name of a player, who must take over the narration for a few seconds while continuing to move in slow motion. In this way, you can make the game a little more difficult.

The **Interview**

Props: video camera with tripod, television and VCR, videotapes of interviews on news shows and talk shows, chairs, theatrical lighting (optional)

Players can have great fun interviewing each other, especially if they throw themselves into the roles of interviewer and interviewee. The objective of a TV interviewer is simply stated: extracting as much information as possible from the interviewee. Some interviewers are confrontational, asking surprise questions and pointing out inconsistencies; others try to ingratiate themselves with the interviewee, hoping to draw out confidences. An interviewee's aims can be more varied: promoting herself or a project, putting the best spin possible on a bad situation, or persuading the audience to agree with her viewpoint.

First Session: In advance, videotape excerpts from a few interviews on varied news and talk shows. Show players the tape and have them discuss the interview styles they observe. Divide the group into pairs, each including one interviewer and one interviewee. The interviewee should take on the role of a prominent person, real or imaginary: a movie star, head of state, business mogul, and so on; in short, a person who is remarkable for her conspicuous behavior and appearance, positive or negative. Encourage the interviewee to consider the following:

- What kind of impression do you want to make on the audience?

- What do you hope to communicate?

- What do you have to hide? How will you handle questions you don't want to answer?

The interviewer should consider the following:

- What do you want to know from the interviewee?

- How do you begin the interview? Do you go straight to the heart of the subject or do you dance around with innocent-sounding questions and set a trap for the interviewee?

- Avoid questions that can be answered "yes" or "no." Use "how" and "why" questions to encourage the interviewee to talk as much as possible.

- End the interview after about 5 minutes. How do you round off the interview? Do you thank the interviewee? Do you sum up what you have learned?

Give players time to think over their roles and plan the interview.

Second Session: Create an interview set with chairs and (if possible) special lighting. Focus a video camera on the set and either operate it yourself or have a volunteer do so. Have pairs practice their interviews and then take turns taping their interviews on the set. Encourage players to stay in character and continue to see each other as interviewer and interviewee, not just as players in a pair. Ask players to go into their roles deeply and to expect the same of their partners.

Save the videotaped interviews and play them for the group in a later session. (Many people feel uncomfortable and self-conscious watching a videotape of what they just finished doing: A waiting period makes watching the tape easier.)

Morphing Games

We often think of morphing as uncanny and inhuman—werewolves, aliens, and insects morph, not humans. But to morph is simply to change, and we are changing all the time. A teenager is in the process of morphing from a child into an adult. Morphing is an everyday occurrence: We might act and dress one way at school or work and act and dress a very different way at a party or at the mall.

Morphing games require players to change their roles, thoughts, or aims in the middle of the game. This stimulates the imagination and takes a scene in unexpected directions that players might not explore otherwise. Players may discover that others interpret the same assignment in different, surprising ways. Players must remain open to a wide range of possibilities in order to transform themselves.

A number of these games require lots of space: Each player needs enough space to carry out the exercises without impinging on others.

Sport
Changes

Props: an audio system and some background music

Have players spread out around the room. Name a sport for players to mime. Encourage them to think of all the different motions that are involved in playing that particular sport. Ask players to mime that sport silently, without using words or sounds. After a minute or so, switch to another sport: football, gymnastics, swimming, hockey, baseball, basketball, soccer, etc. You could mention any sport familiar enough for players to mime its movements. Background music may help players to concentrate. You might choose a fast or a slow tempo, depending on whether you want to focus on energy or precision.

Variations:

* Have players make a gradual transition from one sport to the next. For example, hockey might morph into baseball: The hockey stick slowly rises up and turns into a swinging bat. This exercise is more interesting if players make the movements in slow motion.

* For variation, you can let players add sounds. Slow movements with slow-motion sounds (think of a movie being played back slowly, with distorted sounds) can be great fun for children.

The Route

This game invites players to imagine themselves in different environments and to mime appropriate postures and movements. This experience can be useful as players move on to perform scenes: Any scene has a setting, and this game helps players learn to bring that setting to life.

Have players spread out and close their eyes. Ask players to stay in their places, but to pretend they are making a journey through the different spaces you will mention. Encourage players to explore the environments at every level—both high and low. Point out that players will need to adapt their postures and movements for each space. Narrate a route such as the following:

> *You are wandering through a busy shopping mall and you have to squeeze your way slowly and carefully past several displays of fragile objects. You get into the elevator, which gets fuller and fuller: You are squashed in next to a woman with a baby stroller, and you have to lean precariously to one side to make room. You emerge from the elevator and find yourself on a broad sidewalk. You realize you are late for your train, and run down the steps to the crowded platform, where you push past people to catch your train, but the only space left is in the baggage car between piles of suitcases that are threatening to topple over. Luckily, you wake up in a grassy meadow where you can stretch out luxuriously.*

After the exercise, ask how players imagined the environments and what pleasant or unpleasant experiences they had. If the group is too large, half of them can move while the others watch.

Variation: The same exercise can also be done to music and with the eyes open, moving round the room. Don't change the scenes too quickly, or players may become distracted and collide. Drawing a path on the floor with chalk can be helpful for younger children.

Where Are You?

Certain places have specific actions that are associated with them: We paddle in a swimming pool, steer in a car, and cook in a kitchen.

Have players spread out around the room. Explain that you will mention different locations, and players should use gestures to show the kinds of activities people do in each place. During the course of the game, name several unrelated spaces with special characteristics: a skating rink, the circus, a swimming pool, a dark forest, a rowboat, a dance club, and so on. Encourage players to switch their actions as soon as a new place is mentioned.

Glass Slippers
and Giants' Boots

In advance, search various fairy tales and other stories for short passages about interesting footwear. "Cinderella," "Puss in Boots," and "The Red Shoes" are obvious choices, but you might look through other tales for a giant's enormous boots, a hero's magical flying shoes, and so on.

Read the passages aloud and ask players to move around as if they are wearing the shoes mentioned in the story. Encourage players to change their way of walking as soon as you describe a new kind of footwear. If you notice a player portraying a certain shoe especially well, invite her to come to the front and show off her shoes to the group.

Fashion Show

Point out to the group that people wear very different kinds of clothing for different occasions. How do people dress to go to a party? To play touch football? To fight a fire? Point out that a person wearing a heavy coat moves differently than a person wearing a bathing suit.

Have players sit in a line at the side of the room. Name a situation (for example, a fancy party) and describe an appropriate outfit. These are imaginary clothes that players will make "visible" to the others by the way they move. Ask two players from opposite ends of the line to come out and walk towards each other, modeling the outfit you have described. They should use their motions to show what kind of clothing they are wearing, and what situation they are in. Have pairs of players take turns modeling as you go on to call out the names of a wide variety of outfits: beachwear, wedding clothes, skiwear, a firefighter's gear, and so on. You can add to the fun by switching the outfits in the middle of some players' turns. Can the others see how the clothes are worn? Are the pleats in the wedding veil falling correctly? If a player wants to add something, he can, for instance, jump up and carry the train of the wedding dress or pass someone a hat.

Variation: In advance, ask players to clip magazine or newspaper photos of different kinds of clothing and bring them in as examples.

Dress Each Other

Like game 25 (Fashion Show), this game involves invisible costumes. Divide the group into pairs. Explain that one partner will help the other to dress. The helper passes the clothes and the other partner puts them on. Everything is done in silence. The helper is not allowed to say aloud what clothing he is passing to his partner, but his movements should make it obvious. For instance, he can use his hands to suggest the shape and feel of the clothes. After a few minutes of dressing, the helper can ask his partner what she is wearing: a cowboy outfit, an astronaut's suit, royal robes? Then have partners switch roles and play again.

Variation: Allow the helper to talk as he dresses his partner, but not specifically to describe the clothes. Instead, the helper can talk his partner into the role by telling her what she will have to do in her new job.

Time Warp

People change drastically over time. If we speed up the changes, we can watch the metamorphosis occur.

Have players spread out so that they have space to move around. Ask them to act out a simple series of movements: For example, players pretend to hear the school bell ring, grab their bags, and walk out of the classroom. Now have players repeat the series over and over as you call out different moments in time—for example: You are a baby who can barely walk, you are 90 years old, you are your parents' age, you are living in the future and wearing anti-gravity boots, you are a prehistoric cave dweller, and so on. Players must change their style of moving to match the time you name. Point out that an old person of 90 moves very differently than a teenager, who moves very differently than a baby.

Career Shift

Different jobs always fascinate children. Who doesn't want to hang on the back of a fire engine, drive a tractor, or knead gooey dough in the bakery? An actor's job is to bring other jobs to life, so that the audience can smell the bread baking in the imaginary oven.

Have players spread out and find spaces. Begin by miming a job you enjoy. Point out the small but characteristic gestures that show the audience what job you are doing. Invite players to join you. Name a different job, and begin miming it with players. Try to make the transition from one job to the next seamless: Link the actions together so that one job grows out of the other. As soon as players have the hang of it, drop out. Explain that you will name a different job every minute or so, and they must mime the appropriate characteristics, without using words.

Example: The "bakers" are putting bread in the oven. You call out "janitor" and the bread might turn into a bucket of soapy water as players start mopping the floor. You call out "surgeon" and the big rubber gloves are changed for tight ones as the mop turns into a scalpel....

In a Manner of Speaking

The same person may use dramatically different voices in different situations: She may whisper in fear, shout in jubilation, or snap in annoyance. In this game, players perform short monologues in which they portray characters whose voices and manners change over the course of the scene. In preparation for this game, encourage players to observe people they know and people they see on the street and notice how their voices and manners vary. They can use their observations as inspiration for the monologues.

Before players begin, perform one or two example monologues yourself to demonstrate.

Example 1: On a train, an older aristocratic woman cannot find a seat. No one stands up for her. She begins by asking for a seat in a normal voice. When no one responds, she raises her voice, scolding the others for not yielding their seats. As the woman becomes more and more agitated, her voice becomes increasingly angry, loud, and harsh, and her way of moving is correspondingly different, with more extravagant gestures.

Example 2: A man on a business trip groggily answers the phone in the middle of the night. He scolds the hotel manager for waking him up. His voice takes on a tone of worry when he hears the reason is an

urgent call from his wife. After his wife gets on the phone, the businessman begins shouting in jubilation: Their baby has just been born. The businessman asks to talk to the baby, and he begins cooing tenderly into the phone.

Ask each player to think up a situation in which a character's voice and manner would change: A character might become more and more annoyed, realize he is falling in love, or discover that he's won the lottery. Give players some time to work out their monologues and practice them. (Explain that the monologues can be very brief—30 seconds is plenty of time.) Then invite volunteers to take turns acting them out for the group. Encourage players to make both their voices and movements change with the mood of the scene.

Out of Uniform

We expect people doing certain jobs to dress in a particular way. It's funny to think of a cowpoke in a ballet costume, an office worker in overalls and a hard hat, or a truck driver in a business suit. In this game, teams act out skits in which switches in "uniform" play an important role—a worker is dressed in the wrong clothes, and this causes all kinds of confusion and complications.

Provide players with the following example: A janitor is cleaning up backstage after a rock concert, and she secretly tries on the rock star's costume. Kidnappers sneak in and, thinking the janitor is the rock star, drag her away. Meanwhile, the rock star (who has seen everything) disguises herself in the janitor's uniform to chase the kidnappers and help rescue the janitor.

Divide the group into teams and ask each team to think up a skit along these lines. After 20 minutes of practice, invite teams to perform their skits for the group.

Observation Games

Our eyes are open all day, but how much do we really see? Can players remember the color of the school building? what outfits their best friends are wearing today? the number of steps they climb to get to class? Sight is a gift, but observation is an art.

Observing, listening, noticing, and remembering are important skills that we can develop through practice. The games in this section help players focus on truly observing what they see. In these games, players must observe people, actions, or objects and then use their observations as the basis of a guess, a discussion, or an imitation. Many of the games require players to mirror actions at the moment they see them, linking observation and action.

The observation games work best in silence. Help players to concentrate by creating a peaceful, focused atmosphere and discouraging unnecessary talk. However, feel free to encourage players from the sidelines: Your words of support will help them persevere.

Through the Camera's Lens

Props: a cardboard tube from a toilet paper roll for each pair of players

Paradoxically, limiting our field of vision can make us better observers. In this game, players look through toilet paper tubes, so that they can observe only a small area at any given time. Divide the group into pairs, and give each pair a tube. Have one partner look through the tube. Ask the other partner to choose an emotion—happy, disappointed, miserable, surprised, and so on. She should move around the room, using her expression and movements to show the emotion. Meanwhile, her partner follows her around, watching her through the tube, as if it were a video camera. After a couple of minutes, have partners switch roles and play again. When the game is over, have players discuss the following:

- what emotions they observed

- how they were able to recognize an emotion

- whether the whole body was used to express an emotion

- which parts of the body showed an emotion most clearly

Some parts of the body are much more expressive than others. Older players can discover a lot about themselves and each other with this exercise.

Variation: Instead of having players work in pairs, you could ask one player to stand in the center of the room and mime an emotion. The others look to see the telltale signs of the emotion. The first one to identify the emotion or to ask a question about the emotion then goes to the center and shows how *he* would express that emotion. After this, the emotion can be changed. Save this variation for groups with plenty of experience in observing each other.

Back Talk

Emotions show up clearly on our faces. It is simple to face someone and communicate happiness, sadness, or anger. To communicate the same things with your back turned is somewhat more difficult. Still, a person with hunched shoulders and bowed head looks sad, even from behind.

Divide the group into pairs. Ask them to practice showing five to ten different emotions, without using words or sounds. Partners can take turns acting out emotions and observing. They should give each other feedback on how to show each emotion most effectively. Now have them repeat the same exercise, but focus on how each emotion looks from behind. Encourage players to use their whole body—the posture of the torso, as well as their arms and legs—to express each emotion. Can partners recognize the emotions from behind? Which emotions are the easiest to identify? It is great fun to let volunteers show their efforts to the whole group.

The Mirror

Divide the group into pairs. Have partners stand face to face. Partner A should begin the game as a person looking into a mirror; partner B is his reflection. Partner A initiates movements and partner B mirrors them back. Encourage players to try to move almost simultaneously. After a few minutes, have partners switch roles.

If you like, you can add music to stimulate movement.

Variation (for older players): Instead of trying to move simultaneously with partner A, partner B delays her imitation slightly. Partner A sees B moving as if in a delayed-action shot. B tries to be as careful as possible in copying A. To A, this becomes a replay of his own movements.

Who Is
the Mirror?

Have players practice game 34 (The Mirror) until they are very comfortable mirroring each other. Now ask pairs to try standing side by side and using peripheral vision to mirror each other. Partners should take turns leading and following.

After a few minutes of practice, invite pairs to perform for the whole group. Challenge the group to guess which partner is leading and which is creating the reflection.

Equality

Have players spread out around the room so that they have plenty of room to move and then turn to face you. If there is enough room, have players space themselves side by side in a single line. Turn your back on players and begin making large, simple movements for them to follow. Repeat each movement several times before transforming the movement gradually into a new one. After a few minutes of practice, invite a volunteer to step forward and take over the movements while you step aside. Encourage new players to step forward and take over every minute or two. Ask leaders to repeat their movements and let each movement flow slowly into the next.

Play the game a second time, but without leaders. Start the group off with a simple movement. Challenge the group to observe each other well and follow the flow of movement. Point out that changes in the group movement seem to happen on their own, without an obvious leader initiating them. Watch the group and encourage the players to focus their concentration on one another's movements.

Rewind

This game helps players train their memory for movement. Divide the group into pairs. Ask each player to think of a simple action, such as opening a door and entering a room. Have partners take turns performing and observing as they practice their actions, first in forward motion, and then in reverse—for example, going out of the door backwards, closing the door, and walking away backwards. This should look just like rewinding a videotape. During the practice phase of this game partners should watch each other closely and remind each other of any movements they have forgotten to include as they perform their actions in reverse.

After 10 minutes of practice, invite each of the players to perform their actions in reverse for the rest of the group.

Quick Changes

Ask players to take a good look at you and try to remember the details of how you are dressed. Now have players turn around and close their eyes. Change one small but clearly visible aspect of your appearance: Take off your sweater or glasses, put your hair in a barrette, switch your watch to the opposite wrist, whatever comes to mind. Have players turn around and look again. Challenge them to identify what has changed.

Now divide the group into two roughly equal teams and have the teams line up facing each other. Ask one team to study the other team carefully, and then turn their backs while the other team works together to make two changes—for example, one player might turn his sweater inside out, while two other players switch places in line. Can the other team identify the changes? Have the teams switch roles and play again.

Variation: For older players, the number of changes can be increased. You can add to the fun by bringing hats, sunglasses, newspapers to read, and other extra objects for players to use in making their changes.

Forgotten Items

Props: a variety of objects; a tray to hold them; a cloth to cover them; and a stopwatch or clock with second hand

In advance, gather lots of different objects—ordinary household items and perhaps some unusual objects as well. Arrange the objects on a large tray and cover it with a cloth. Divide the group into teams of about four players. Lift the cloth and display the objects for 10 seconds (or a different fixed amount of time). Ask players to observe the objects carefully. Now cover the objects and challenge each team to work together to list what was on the tray.

Collect the lists and make a note of the objects that each team forgot. These objects will become the starting point for a sketch. Ask each team to make up a short play, using as props some of the objects they forgot to list. (There will be some overlap in the forgotten objects—simply choose a few different objects for each group.) After 20 minutes of practice, invite the teams to perform their sketches for the rest of the group.

The Secret Leader

Have everyone stand in a circle. Join the circle and make a series of motions for players to imitate. Encourage players to follow the changes in motion quickly, so that the circle moves almost simultaneously.

Now ask one player to stand outside the door and wait until you bring her back in. While she is out of the room, choose a new leader to take over initiating the movements. Encourage the others to follow the leader closely, but try not to look at him directly. Now bring the player who went outside back into the room. After watching the circle for a while, can she guess who the leader is? Ask another player to leave the room and choose a new leader for the next round.

Be Something

Props: one object brought in by each player; a large cardboard box

In advance, ask each player to bring in a small object. It can be anything—an orange, a book, a baseball, a stapler. Arrange all the objects on a desk or table. Have players form pairs and choose one object to study. Encourage them to consider what it looks like, how it is shaped, what it is made of, how it works, what it is used for, how it can move, and what it feels like: hard, floppy, brittle, spongy, rubbery, and so on.

After a few minutes, collect all the objects and hide them in a closed box. Now challenge each pair to work together to portray their chosen object through mime. Encourage partners to "become" the object itself, rather than pretending to hold or use it. After 10 minutes of practice, invite each pair to present their mime portrait of the object to the group. Can the others recognize what object the partners are pretending to be?

Trust Games

Actors must trust each other. If they do not, they cannot open up and create honest, intimate performances. Most of the games in this book will not work well unless there is mutual trust between the players. Supporting other players, leaning on others for support, and resisting the urge to make fun of each other are all skills that need to be developed and practiced. The games in this section help players learn to trust.

In some of these games, players do more than trust each other from a distance. Some games call for players to touch each other, or hold each other, so they need to act seriously. This can be difficult for teenagers and older children. Their first reaction to being asked to hold hands, for instance, will usually be to start giggling and joking around. In our culture, people rarely touch each other except in a sexual or violent context—or in sports. Nervous giggling and jokes reflect players' insecurity about touching. Allow players to get this out of their systems, but quickly guide them to focus on the assignment. Of course, it is absolutely essential to put a stop to any harassing talk or touching immediately, or trust will be shattered.

Intimacy is an integral part of acting, and trust games can help players get over their shyness. Trust games are useful for teenage actors uncomfortable with the idea of acting out a stage kiss, for example. With practice, players can trust each other enough to recognize that a touch does not have to be sexual or violent: It can simply be an offer of support from a friend and fellow actor.

pairs

Air
Pressure

Ask a volunteer to help you demonstrate the game. Face the volunteer and hold your hands out in front, palms facing forward. Have the volunteer hold out his hands so that your palms are almost touching, but not quite. Ask the volunteer to follow your lead as you stand in place and make a few simple movements with your arms. As you move, keep your palms close together, but never let them touch.

Now divide the group into pairs and have partners explore moving with their hands almost touching. Ask players to move without speaking. Point out the tension that players feel between their hands: It feels like air pressure, like a balloon pressed between their hands. Encourage players to concentrate on this feeling.

Afterwards, invite players to discuss how they experienced the feeling of "air pressure." This is a game that can be played over and over. Each time, encourage players to deepen their level of concentration.

Body Tension

Like game 42 (Air Pressure), this game makes use of the "air pressure" between two bodies. Have pairs of players move as close together as they can without touching. There should always be an inch or two of space between partners' bodies. Pairs might begin by moving their sides together, then carefully rotate until they are back to back, front to front, and so on. Encourage partners to imagine the cushion of air between their bodies and maintain the same small distance between them at all times. Ask pairs to play the game silently. You may want to play tranquil classical or new age music to help players concentrate.

Out of Thin Air

Divide the group into pairs. Ask partners to hold out their hands and pretend they are holding something between them. The imaginary object can start out as an undefined shape.

Invite partners to take turns using mime to develop a part of the object—perhaps one partner uses hand movements to show that the object has a flat, smooth top, and the other partner mimes twisting dials on its front. Players should not talk, but they can make sound effects if they wish. Taking cues from each other, partners work together to "discover" what it is they are holding. They both hold the imaginary object at all times so that the "air pressure" is always there between the players. See game 42 (Air Pressure) for more on this concept. After a few minutes, ask each pair to explain what it is that they are holding.

Air and Balance

Ask a volunteer to help you demonstrate a balancing pose. You and the volunteer should stand with your foreheads touching, feet slightly apart, arms straight out, and palms touching. Begin shuffling your feet backward, so that you are farther and farther apart. Lean on each other for balance. Point out that the two of you are balancing together. Now move your feet back in a bit toward your partner and try to move your palms slightly apart—creating an air cushion of about two inches between them—while still leaning inward and balancing. Move your feet a bit more if parting your palms is too difficult.

Divide the group into pairs. Ask partners to work together to create a different balance. Perhaps they could hold only one hand together, or they could lean back-to-back. Have partners first practice balancing together while touching. Then have them try to maintain a balance with each other without actually touching, but still almost touching, as they move. Point out that partners should keep a very small distance between them, but it is as if they touch and lean on each other. This creates a different kind of balance, with a slight air barrier between them. Balance can even be achieved on one leg: When firmly planted on the standing leg, partners can make a pose with the free leg.

Spotters

Tell players that when gymnasts are learning new moves, coaches "spot" them—hold or support them to prevent dangerous falls. Explain that players will form teams and try out balancing positions while their teammates act as spotters. Divide the group into teams of five or more. In each team, one person stands in the center and the others gather round him and hold him gently by the shoulders, wrists, or back. The center player should be able to move easily, but should also feel supported. He tries out various balancing positions: standing on one leg with the other stretched out behind, leaning to one side, and so on. The others make sure he doesn't fall. Ask players to refrain from unnecessary talking. The spotters especially should refrain from making suggestions or comments to the center player and should limit themselves to questions such as: *Is this loose enough? Which way are you going to move now?*

After a minute or two, ask the spotters to let go of the center player. They should remain gathered around him and touch him only if he needs support. This is a game of give-and-take. Keep playing the game until all the team members have taken a turn in the center.

Soloist and Group

This is a good game to play after game 46 (Spotters). As in Spotters, a central player is surrounded by teammates. This time, the teammates are far from passive helpers: Now they control the movements.

Divide the group into teams of about five and have team members draw straws to choose a soloist. Assign each group a situation with plenty of movement to act out: an earthquake, a car race, a storm-tossed boat, a whitewater-rafting trip, and so on. The soloist is the only team member portraying a human in the skit. Her teammates play the wind, the waves, the earthquake, and so on. The soloist narrates the action, and her teammates create all the appropriate chaos, motion, and sound effects. For instance, when the soloist says, "Oh, no! The ground is starting to shake!" her teammates hold her arms and legs and jiggle her, while they make the rumbling sounds of an earthquake. Keep an eye on groups to make sure the game does not get out of hand: The soloist should feel safe at all times. Encourage players to stay in character—particularly the soloist. Teams should draw out their skits for several minutes, until the soloist wraps things up: "Phew! The quake is over."

Each team can practice by themselves and then do short performances for the rest of the group.

Energy Games

The games in this section involve miming energy—weight, lightness, power, and force. It can be difficult to convince an audience you are carrying a heavy weight when your hands are empty, but this is a very useful skill in drama. Even in a fully-staged show with sets and props, actors must use their imaginations: They must be freezing cold under the hot lights, strain under the weight of a boulder made of styrofoam, or be buffeted by a violent storm represented by lighting and an offstage fan. Communicating this energy to the audience is essential to a powerful, convincing performance. In this context, energy is both power and weight, tension and relaxation, breathing and the holding of the breath.

In the energy games, players will learn to feel the weight of an imaginary object, the force of an imaginary earthquake, the pull of other players on an imaginary rope, and the weightlessness of an imaginary walk in space. They will use their experiences to make those imaginary things real to an audience.

Invisible Object

Props: object cards (see below)

In advance, write the names of objects onto notecards. Choose everyday objects that differ in weight and size—for example: skateboard, hot dog, key, suitcase, telephone, newspaper, napkin, ladder, lamp, sleeping bag.

Have players form pairs and ask each pair to pick a card without looking. Invite partners to imagine that together they are holding the object named on their card. Is it big or small, light or heavy, hard or soft, rigid or flexible? Partners should explore different movements they can make with the object—they might mime using it in ordinary ways and then experiment with other ways it might be used. Partners could pass the object back and forth or work together to hold and use it. As they experiment with the object, partners can discuss how it could be incorporated into a story. What might someone do with this object? What problems could it cause or solve? Have pairs work together to develop a short mime scene (without words) in which something happens with the object. After 10 or 15 minutes of practice, ask pairs to present their mimes to the group.

Example: Two aliens find a skateboard and try to figure out what it is. They try using it as a hat, a communication device, and a stool, at which point they discover it rolls. Now that they know the board is for transportation, they try riding it. The aliens fall a few times, but quickly get the hang of skateboarding and try a few tricks.

Partners must focus their concentration on each other. Together, they have to bring the object to life and embellish the story. This requires cooperation and careful use of energy during the game.

Variation: Once you have practiced the game in this way, you can use it as a warm-up in a future session and continue with a game that uses dialog.

Weightless

In this game, players practice moving as if they were as light as a feather. This teaches them to keep their energy streaming at a constant level through the course of a scene. The game also helps players develop their breathing processes.

In advance, choose a scenario involving weightlessness (or near weightlessness): riding in a spaceship, walking on the moon, scuba diving, or parachute jumping, for instance. Decide carefully how you will describe the scene to the group. Have players spread out around the room. Begin with a breathing exercise. Ask players to breathe in through the nose and out through the mouth. For a minute or two, let players concentrate on their breathing in silence. Then invite players to imagine that they are weightless, like an astronaut in space who can float and drift at will. Now explain that you will tell a story, and they should act it out. Encourage players to move on each exhalation of breath, and pause as they inhale.

Give a moment-by-moment account of the scene, reminding players to perform every movement as if they were weightless. For example, you might narrate as follows: "Get ready, the story is about to begin. Breathe in. . . . Breathe out. . . . It's a bumpy landing on the moon. You grab your safety harness for support. Now you unstrap your harness and float toward the hatch. . . ."

Heavy as Lead

Props: a few heavy objects, such as a bag full of books or a rock

Invite players to pretend they are lifting a heavy object. This is harder than it sounds: It can be very difficult to make it look as if you are burdened with a heavy load when all you have in your hands is thin air. Players might find the mime easier if they hold an actual heavy object first. Encourage players to pick up one of the prop objects and feel how heavy it is. (Make sure players bend their knees and lift the objects with their legs, so as not to injure their backs.) After all of the players have lifted a heavy object, have them use that experience to create a realistic mime of weight. Players can practice "lifting" all kinds of imaginary objects.

Now have players sit down in a line or a big circle. Ask them to get up one by one and do the following mime: Pick up an imaginary heavy object, carry it a short distance, put it down, and then smash it to pieces. Each player can decide what his imaginary object will be. Encourage players to use their faces as well as their bodies to demonstrate the object's weight. Can the other group members identify what the object is and estimate how heavy it is?

small
groups

Tug-of-War

In game 50 (Heavy as Lead), players tackle the difficult task of lifting an imaginary object and showing its weight. Tug-of-War adds the challenge of sharing the imaginary burden with others. Players must work dynamically as a team to show how the tension and weight shift. They must feel not only the weight of the imaginary object, but also the force and energy exerted by their teammates.

Divide the group into teams of about five players. Assign to each team a scenario in which weight and effort are central—for example: playing tug-of-war, pushing a stalled car, carrying a sofa upstairs, and so on. (Older, more experienced groups might come up with their own scenarios.) Everyone should help carry the weight or help pull the rope. Encourage players to explore how the weight can shift: What would happen if a player were to let go of one end of the sofa or rope? The mime can include sounds, but there should be no dialog. After about 15 minutes of practice, let teams perform their mimes for the rest of the group.

Variation: Repeat the game, but this time allow teams to include dialog.

Feel the Motion

Game 51 (Tug-of-War) involves moving a weight as a team. This time, players will not move an object: The object will move them.

Divide the group into teams of about four players each. Each team will act out a situation in which people are moved by objects and forces—for example: flying a plane through heavy turbulence, riding in bumper cars, riding a roller-coaster, sliding down a hill on a toboggan, and so on. Depending on the age and experience of the group, you might assign situations or let teams come up with their own. After about 10 minutes of discussion and practice, have teams act out their situations for the rest of the group, using shouts or sounds, if desired, but no dialog.

This game could be adapted to create a situation game: The object could create a tricky situation for the players (see Situation Games, page 66).

Joints

Actors need to be conscious of their movements while performing. This game helps players focus on what parts of the body they are moving and why they move that way.

Have players spread out around the room and close their eyes. You may want to play music to set the mood. Explain that you will tell a story, and they should act it out. Ask players to listen carefully as you annouce each joint that will need to move. You could use one of the examples below, or perhaps tell a story involving a dream, astronauts, or a fantasy machine.

Example 1: You have been captured by a gigantic spider who has paralyzed you and wrapped you in a cocoon of thread. The paralysis is beginning to wear off. You try moving your eyelids and mouth, then roll your neck to make sure it is working. You turn your head to the left and notice that your left arm is sticking out of the thread. You begin by wiggling your fingers, then rotate your wrist. Now you have enough movement in the arm to bend your left elbow and start using your fingers to pull the sticky thread off your right arm....

Example 2 (for younger children): You are marionettes, lying flopped on the floor where the puppeteer has left you. Now that the puppeteer is gone, you decide to move on your own. First you stretch one arm: Slowly and sequentially, move your fingers, wrist, elbow, and shoulder. Then you decide to stand up. The first time, it doesn't work....

Encourage players to keep moving through every bone and muscle: This will increase the power of their portrayals.

Situation Games

Our daily lives are full of rich material for actors and scriptwriters. Many routine situations beg to be turned into a sketch or play.

In a crowded store at holiday time, for instance, there are always people who want to push to the front of the line. A dramatic scene with this setting would reveal all sorts of interesting aspects of human nature: selfishness, impatience, greed, and more of those unattractive personal traits that surface when people find themselves in a difficult situation. The games in this section invite players to act out common situations that any of us might find ourselves in: sitting in a doctor's waiting room, going to a family party, or standing in a grocery line.

small
groups

The Waiting Room

Props: a few chairs

There are all kinds of waiting rooms, rooms in which people wait to see the doctor, dentist, or veterinarian; to be interviewed for a job; to audition for a play; even to appear on a television talk show. In a waiting room, you can feel insecurity, confidence, anxiety, hope, relief, or disappointment.

Arrange a few chairs in one area and have the group sit on the floor facing them. For the first round, tell the group what sort of a waiting room this will be. Call on players one by one to enter the waiting room and take a seat. Encourage them to start up a conversation in which it becomes clear why each of them has come. If necessary, act as narrator and make suggestions about the different characters' motivations. Suggest a problem that might develop: perhaps the appointments are running behind schedule or one character tries to jump ahead in line? Encourage players to come up with

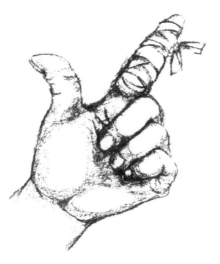

problems and move toward solutions—positive or negative. You might act as the secretary/doctor and usher players into the office (and out of the game) periodically, at which point other players could enter the waiting room.

Once players have the idea of the game, divide the group into teams of about five players. Ask each team to make up its own waiting room scenario and act it out for the group.

Variation: Invite each player to make up her own reason for being in the waiting room: Perhaps the first player to enter is waiting for a doctor's appointment, while the next player is waiting to audition for a circus act. Each player creates her own part of the story and decides when to leave the room. After a few minutes, you might choose one player to play the secretary role and usher players into the office. What kind of waiting room does this turn out to be? How does this affect the players who find they are in the wrong waiting room? Encourage the secretary to steer the game along and resolve the conflicting situations.

The Party

Tell the group that this game is about a party, and they will play the partygoers. Have players sit in a semicircle facing an open space. Choose one player to be the host. He begins the game on stage alone, and others will gradually join him.

The host shows everyone what kind of party this will be, perhaps by idly talking to himself as he makes the final arrangements, or by having a phone conversation. Is it a class reunion? A family reunion? A baby shower? A party in honor of a graduate? The party begins slowly: Other players should enter singly or in pairs. Make sure players allow enough time between entrances for each guest to establish her identity.

Once all the guests have arrived, a problem arises: Perhaps an uninvited guest shows up, someone bursts into tears, or someone acts so obnoxiously that he offends everyone. (If players need help coming up with a problem, make suggestions.) This problem will disturb the whole proceedings and eventually break the party up.

It is an art to carry a supporting role through from start to finish because it is very challenging to act out a subtle role that adds to overall atmosphere and doesn't detract the audience's attention away from the character whose role should be the primary focus. If the game gets out of hand, pause the action. Change something or add a new element, so that the game will take a new direction. Eventually, players will learn to master the game and handle the tension.

 small groups

The End

Props: a timer or stopwatch; story cards (see below)

In drama games, nothing is preordained: Any scene could go in countless different directions. This game invites players to explore some of those alternate possibilities. In advance, write on notecards the titles of stories you know are familiar to the group: books or plays that were discussed in class, fairy tales, or movies everyone has seen. Divide the group into teams of about four players and pass out a card to each team. Have teams think about how their story ends. How could the story end differently? Each team should make up two alternate endings—perhaps a sad story could end happily, a crucial decision could be changed, or the characters could end up doing something completely different. Have teams develop both alternative endings into quick 60-second sketches and rehearse them for 10 or 15 minutes. Then ask each team to perform an ending for the group while you time the performance. Ask the audience whether they want to let that ending stand, or see a different ending. If the group wants a different ending, the team performs its second alternate ending.

Example: In the story of *Romeo and Juliet,* Romeo kills himself because he is fooled by Juliet's faked death; when Juliet awakens and sees his body, she kills herself. A team might develop one skit in which Romeo delays killing himself and discovers that Juliet is alive; and another skit in which Juliet, finding Romeo has killed himself for love, resolves not to make that mistake herself, and lives on sadder but wiser.

Variation: Ask experienced teams to quickly make up or improvise a dramatic scene and act it out. When the scene is over, ask the audience if it wants to see a different ending. If it does, the team must make up a new ending on the spot. This variation is exciting because teams must cooperate well and think on their feet.

Secret Instructions

Props: "secret instruction" cards (see below)

Save this game for groups who have mastered other situation games, such as game 56 (The End). This situation game includes a twist: As players act out their scene, you will periodically hand secret instructions to various players. In advance, prepare notecards with dramatic instructions such as:

- Your cell phone rings: Your brother is being dragged off to jail.

- You're wearing a walkman. Start humming and gradually sing louder and louder.

- Start an argument with someone in the room.

- Pick someone's pocket.

- You are falling in love with someone in the room.

Begin the game by providing a setting and a situation. For example, players might be waiting on a rainy train platform, huddled together in a shelter; the train is late.

After a few seconds, hand the first instruction card to one of the players. This player should read the card silently and act out the instruction as soon as possible. The players then react to the new situation. Hand out instructions periodically to different players, until the scene reaches a climax. Then begin again with a new situation.

Set Designer

Props: a great many objects large and small, including furniture, fabric, household items, toy food, party decorations, and just about anything

In advance, create as many sets and gather as many props as you can: portable furniture; household objects such as dishware, plastic flowers, and costume jewelry; and so on. Many effects can be created by draping fabric.

Invite players to design a stage set of their own. Have the group sit in a semicircle in front of a stage or performance area that is as bare and neutral as possible. Have players come forward one by one and add a piece of furniture or a prop to the set, which will slowly take on a certain character. This game can be repeated several times with different props, so that the players begin with normal situations and then begin making more absurd ones.

Players might build up a family living room, a club on New Year's Eve, or a haunted house. Once the scenery meets with everyone's approval, a dialog game can begin (see Dialog Games, page 73).

Dialog Games

A dialog is a spoken conversation between two people. This series of games provides players with opportunities to practice improvising dialogs, writing dialog scripts, and acting out scripted dialogs. These games will work more smoothly if players have experience with improvisation games.

When two players are performing a dialog, make sure that the audience does not interrupt. Each dialog should progress to a clear ending: A problem develops at the beginning of the dialog, and it is solved by the end. In many television shows, dialog often begins, develops, and ends in just a couple of shots. Many dialogs last no more than a minute. Encourage players to use short sentences in dialogs, and to bring each dialog to a quick conclusion.

Moods

This is a short game to help players practice using their voices to express different moods. Seat the group in a half circle. Tell players you will call them forward one by one to speak a line, using their tone of voice and gestures to show a particular emotion. Each player should exaggerate that emotion a little more than the player before. For example, the first player might say, "You borrowed my car?" in a tone of mild surprise. The second player might repeat the line in an incredulous tone; the third in astonishment. Perhaps the fourth player is speechless.

Let players try a whole series of emotions, such as anger, fear, courage, pride, disappointment, and so on.

60

Two Moods

Have the group sit in a semicircle. Call on pairs of players to come forward and perform very brief scenes: only a minute or so each. Assign a situation and two moods to each pair of players. An example situation might be: A mother asks her son to do the dishes, and he says no. The two moods would be anger and defiance. Have players come up two by two to perform different situations and moods until everyone has had a turn.

Now divide the group into teams of about four players. Ask each team to make up a scene that involves two very different moods. Encourage teams to juxtapose completely different types of characters as well. For example, exuberant football fans might interrupt some very dignified opera singers during a performance. After about 10 minutes of practice, invite teams to perform for the whole group.

pairs

Dialog with Soundtrack

Props: sound system and a short musical selection (see below)

In advance, choose a piece of music that has no lyrics, but nevertheless conveys a clear mood. Many pieces of classical music are suitable for this. Select a fragment about 2 minutes long. Play the fragment as the group listens, and ask players what mood they hear. Play the music a second time and invite players to imagine the music is part of a movie soundtrack: What kind of a scene might take place as it plays? Have each player make up a short conversation between two people that fits with this music. Encourage players to incorporate a problem and a resolution in their dialog.

Have players form pairs, discuss their dialog ideas, and practice the scene they feel works best. Play the music several times while players practice, so they can make sure their dialogs fit the mood (and length) of the selection. After 20 minutes, invite pairs to perform for the rest of the group. Play the music softly in the background so that it does not drown out the dialog.

Babble

This game gives players the chance to improvise lines of dialog aloud, without the pressure of others listening. Have players form pairs and sit face-to-face. Tell players that on your signal, they should all start talking to themselves at once. Each player should improvise both sides of a dialog between two characters with different and contrasting moods. Encourage players to use different funny voices for the two characters: Remind them that no one is listening! When you signal again, everyone should stop.

Now have partners describe to each other the conversations they made up. Together, they should decide which scene has the most potential or they can combine elements from both scenes. Have partners develop the scene into a dialog of about 15 lines and then have them rehearse it for about 20 minutes. Then invite pairs to perform their dialogs for the whole group.

Read Between the Lines

Props: dialog sample with multiple copies (see below)

In advance, write a sample dialog such as the one below; be sure its context is never made clear. Make enough copies of the dialog for every player to have one. (You may want to include the writing rules—outlined in the bulleted list below—on the photocopy as well: Players will need them later.)

A: Where were you?

B: I can't tell you.

A: Why not?

B: That's too complicated.

A: Why are you being so mysterious about it?

B: There's a good reason for that.

A: Well, this was fun—see you.

B: Hey, wait! I wanted to ask you. . . . Oh, well.

First session: Hand out the sample dialog. Invite players to imagine who the characters are, what they are talking about, and when and where the conversation takes place. Have players form pairs, rehearse the dialog, and perform it for the group. Partners make up their own context. For example, one pair might be secret agents, while another might include a host who has planned a surprise party and the unsuspecting guest of honor.

Now give players their homework assignment: Write one or more dialogs before the next session. Explain that players can write about whatever they like, but they should try to make their dialogs open to interpretation, just as the sample dialog is. Ask players to follow a few rules in writing:

- do not give the characters names: label them A and B
- do not say where the action takes place
- do not mention time
- do not write more than eight lines of dialog per scene
- make sure the conversation has a definite ending
- use short sentences
- bring two copies of the dialog

Second session: Ask players to clip the two copies of their dialog(s) together (one for each partner in a pair) and place them in a pile. Divide the group into pairs and have each pair select a dialog from the pile. (If players select their own dialog by accident, ask them to choose a different one.) Partners should read the script, make up a context for it, and decide whether or not they can develop it into a performance. Pairs can work with several scripts over the course of the session to see how differently they are written. After about 20 minutes of experimentation and practice, invite each pair to present one dialog to the group.

Action Verbs

This game involves a dialog that is not spoken, but mimed. Have players form pairs and spread out around the room. Partners should stand face-to-face. Ask one partner from each pair to choose and act out an action verb, such as *jump*, *fall*, or *turn*. The other partner should choose another verb associated with the first and act it out. For example, *jump* might be answered with *hop*. Players could also choose more complicated action verbs to mime, such as *bake* or *drive*. Have partners go back and forth, carrying on a conversation in mime.

After partners have gone back and forth a few times, you might invite them to start an "argument" in mime, acting out verbs with opposite (or at least very different) meanings. For instance, *stomp* might be answered with *tiptoe*, which is answered by *smash*, which is answered by *fix*. Discuss afterwards what the different words were and how partners recognized and responded to them.

Writing Games

Many kids think that they can't write. For them, writing seems difficult, frustrating, and doomed to failure. Scripts for sketches and plays can be a fun medium to get these kids excited about writing.

Since scripts are mainly composed of dialog, writing one feels almost like speaking with a pen. Scriptwriters don't have to be so concerned about perfect grammar, because their objective is to reproduce the way people talk. This is not to say that scriptwriting is easy, however. Developing a story in dialog can be a real challenge. These writing games will help inexperienced writers to com-pose a script. The games help players come up with ideas, develop their ideas, and stretch their language and vocabulary skills. Most of the games are designed for older players, but you can easily adapt the games to the age and skill level of a particular group.

Word Game

Scriptwriting can be a daunting task for kids who don't think they have the vocabulary to express themselves. This game helps players realize that they know far more words than they thought they did. Seat players at desks or tables with pen and paper. Write a short sentence on the chalkboard, such as: "The train station is my home."

Divide the group into teams of about four players. Each team writes down a series of words that can be associated with the sentence on the board—for example: *runaway, bench, backpack, rush hour, waiting, trash can, chilly.*

Now ask teams to write a new list of words. If they haven't already, encourage players to think of words that describe emotions and actions. The new list should evoke problems that could happen in the situation described—for example: *hungry, alone, gang, tease, threaten, attack.*

Have teams write one more list of words, this one evoking solutions to the problems described in the second list—for example: *escape, help, telephone, uncle, reunion, train, home.*

Ask the teams to discuss their word lists, make connections between words, and use them as the basis for a short sketch. Is there an obvious main character and supporting role? Where does the action take place? What time is it? Have teams jot down their ideas in story form first, and keep it short—a maximum of 20 lines. Then have them write the scene as a dialog. Point out that people usually speak in short sentences, and encourage teams to keep their dialog sentences short. See Dialog Games, page 73, for more tips on writing dialog.

Headlines

Props: newspapers; scissors

When asked to make up a play, kids often say, "I can't think of a story." This game helps players realize that there are fascinating stories everywhere they look—in their own lives, in the people they pass on the street, and even in the pages of the daily newspapers.

In advance, gather a number of newspapers and ask players to bring in papers as well. Before the first session, search through the paper for a few exciting headlines that leave room for interpretation, such as *Father Claims Daughter Stole Business, Radioactive Pigeons Found Near Power Plant, A Difficult Case,* and *Are Video Cameras Watching You?* Clip only the headlines, so that players cannot see the accompanying stories.

First session: Display the headlines you clipped and invite players to look for other headlines that might form the seeds of interesting plays. Ask players to read only the headlines, not the body text of the stories. Each player should clip her favorite headline.

Have players take notes on developing their headlines into scripts. Ask them to consider the following:

- Who are the main characters: an old man? an ambitious daughter? a hundred cooing pigeons?

- What are the characters like? Include their personalities, ages, jobs, hobbies, and backgrounds, and explain briefly how these factors influence their decisions.

- Where does the action take place: a factory building? an attic room?

- At what time does the action take place: at dinner time? in the middle of the night?

- What is going to happen or has just happened? an argument? a strange discovery? a kidnapping?

Second session: Have players work on writing and revising their scripts. Encourage them to leave plenty of space between the lines as they write or type their script drafts, so that they have room to add or revise material later. Remind them to keep the lines of dialog short. You might have players work in pairs to revise their scripts: Partners could do dramatic readings of the scripts and give each other feedback about the events and dialog.

Variation: Instead of clipping only the headlines, have players clip the accompanying articles as well. Players can read through the articles and run through the questions above to see what elements could be worked into a script.

Write Four Plays at Once!

Sometimes, working on several ideas at once can unlock creativity. Have each player take a sheet of writing paper and fold it in half vertically to form a crease. Point out that the sheet now has four columns, two on one side and two on the other. Suggest four play titles—for example: *Grandpa Explains the Universe, The Interrogation, A Journey to the Unknown,* and *Once Friends, Now Enemies*—and have players write one title at the top of each column.

Ask players to think about each title and make up two characters who could appear in a scene of that name. Each player decides who his characters are, and describes them briefly. For example:

1. Grandpa Explains the Universe	2. The Interrogation
A: old man (76 years old/retired professor of physics) B: grandson (13 years old/potential inventor)	A: criminal (35 years old/specialty is mugging old women) B: detective (32 years old/has mother who has been mugged)

Ask players to start in column 1 and begin writing out the scene in dialog form. After a few minutes, have them switch to column 2 and start that dialog. Every few minutes, signal players to move on to the next column. After column 4, have them continue with column 1. At the end of the session not all the scripts will be finished, but that is not important. In a subsequent session, you might ask players to choose their favorite dialog, complete it, revise it, and develop it into a script that could be performed.

If players act out their scripts in subsequent sessions, have them exchange scripts so that no one is performing his own scene. This makes the game more interesting for both the writer and the actors.

Variation: You can adapt this game for use as an introduction game for groups who don't know each other yet (see Introduction Games, page 8). Arrange desks or tables so that players can pass their scripts around in a large circle. Have players begin the game as above, by writing characters in the columns and beginning the dialog in column 1. At your signal, each player passes her script to the player on her left. This player begins writing the dialog in column 2, using the characters he finds described on the sheet. Players continue switching papers and columns every few minutes. Keep the scripts moving clockwise around the circle, and they will eventually come back to the original writer. How did the scenes develop in the hands of different players? Which ideas might work well in a polished script?

68

The Evening News

Props: video camera and tripod (or cassette player with microphone)

Players are probably familiar with the format of a television news show: The anchor sits at a desk and acts as a kind of host, introducing stories, summing them up, and moving on to the next; correspondents make reports from different places and narrate clips of newsworthy events; the meteorologist gives the weather report; and the sportscaster narrates sports highlights.

Invite players to make up their own news broadcasts. Have the group work together to decide on three or four subjects for news reports (including sports and weather). Encourage players to choose humorous subjects as well as serious ones, so as to make the final presentation more fun. One player should act as director for each news report. Different players can take on the roles of news anchor, correspondents, meteorologist, and sportscaster. Others can be figures in the news: heads of state, protesters, criminals, people displaced by a tornado, basketball players, and so on.

The director of each news report gets together with her correspondent (or meteorologist or sportscaster) and the figures in the news to decide how the story will unfold and to rehearse the various roles involved in the broadcast. The anchor decides in what order the reports will come and makes up lines to introduce each one, sum it up, and segue to the next report. Have the group rehearse the whole broadcast once or twice, and then videotape it.

Variation: Instead of creating a television show, players can make a radio broadcast. Players who are not yet accustomed to acting in public may feel more comfortable with this variation.

Living Video Games

Both young people and old play video games. Mortal Kombat™, Tomb Raider™, and Myst™ are just a few of the thousands of games that keep people glued to the monitor. Nearly all of the members of any group are likely to share this hobby.

There are many different kinds of video games: sports games, adventure games, quiz games, race games, martial arts games, and so on. Many games are about winning or losing, living or dying, scoring points or getting destroyed. The same elements recur in game after game. The figures move according to fixed patterns, make sounds or short speeches, bump into obstacles, end up in tricky situations, and save themselves—or not. As a prelude to playing the games in this section, invite group members to describe their favorite computer games. What elements do they have in common?

The five games in this section can be played one after the other, perhaps in the form of a week of daily classes. These games use video-game conventions to inspire movement, improvisation, and characterization. Players use their bodies and voices to portray a video game in three dimensions. Finally, they design a "living" video game of their own.

69

Locomotion

Props: a sound system; cartoon music (optional)

Nearly every video game involves movement. Characters must walk, run, jump, fall, kick, punch, leap, and so on. Not only that, each character has its own style of moving. One monster lurches around, its enormous bulk wobbling on little crooked legs. A soccer player moves quite differently than a ninja or a zombie. Invite the group to practice moving like the creatures in an imaginary video game. If you wish, have them move to suitable music. The players can move across the room from corner to corner, one by one, so that everyone can see the different "walks." Encourage players to create all kinds of different characters: not only monsters and robots, but also creatures that make supple, fluid movements.

You might have some players repeat their "walks" in slow motion so that everyone can study the series of small movements that make up the larger movement. If players need ideas, you might call out different characters who move in characteristic ways, and let players try out all the walks: giant, elf, football player, royalty, ogre, cat burglar, wrestler, karate expert. Encourage players to vary the speed of their walks, the height of the body, and the power of their gestures, as well as their movements.

Emotions
and Sounds

The characters in the most recent video games are becoming more and more lifelike. Some can show a whole range of emotions with their facial expressions. Others may transform completely when they are in danger. Many characters show emotions with sounds: They can laugh, grunt, scream, speak a short text, and so on. Very often, these sounds occur in a simple, easy-to-remember pattern that players can easily remember.

In advance, ask players if they have favorite video game characters they would like to use in this game. (Usually most of the players will know plenty of video-game heroes and all their characteristics.) If so, players should practice the characters they want to portray, including their sounds and expressions. Players who don't have favorite characters can make up their own—for example: A muscleman who makes all kinds of wild movements but is really terrified of the others and keeps changing his sounds and feelings, from strong to scared.

Divide the group into pairs and have partners work together to develop the sounds and emotions expressed by one or two characters. Encourage partners to give each other feedback.

Obstacles and Pathways

Most video games require players to stay on their toes: If you don't press the "jump" button at the right moment, you might fall into a bottomless pit or be swallowed by a flying shark. Obstacles like these force characters to seek out safe pathways through the game. Different characters in the same game may have special ways of moving and different pathways along which they must move.

Divide the group into teams of about four players. Each team will devise and follow an imaginary circuit around the room, complete with various obstacles and traps. It's not necessary to create an actual obstacle course. Encourage players to show through mime the things they have to clamber over, the pit into which they fall, or how high they have to jump. Point out that video-game characters are much more agile than people: They do things that are impossible in real life. Players can exaggerate their movements wildly and escape unbelievably perilous situations. Making the appropriate sound effects (roaring monsters, rushing water, and so on) will help bring the obstacles to life. If players have developed their own video-game characters during games 69 (Locomotion) and 70 (Emotion and Sounds), invite them to portray these characters as they follow the circuit. Do different characters have to follow different pathways? Do they handle the same obstacle in different ways?

After about 20 minutes of practice, invite teams to perform their circuits for the whole group. Encourage teams to show how various characters move according to their own pattern, come across obstacles, reach the finishing line, or get swallowed up by the monster on the way.

1,000 Lives

Props: a video game and a system on which to play it

In video games, the characters have many lives. They may die in one game, but they'll be back again in the next one. Not all the obstacles are deadly, either: Sometimes they just cause bruises or scorch marks.

Invite players to study an actual video game. Players might run the demonstration/tutorial function, and then play one or two rounds of the game while others look on. Have players discuss the various characters, the sounds and expressions they use to display emotions, the characters' patterns of movement, and the obstacles they encounter.

Now the group will work together to recreate this video game in three dimensions. Some players might act out the role of obstacles in the game, while others act the role of characters. Encourage them to play the game as accurately as possible, and then allow them to decide whether they want to make changes or improvements. Have players portraying obstacles switch roles with players portraying characters in the game. It is especially fun for players to experience "death" in various ways and then get right back up and start playing again.

Game Design

Players developed video-game characters in games 69 (Locomotion) and 70 (Emotions and Sounds). They recreated the structures of video games in games 71 (Obstacles and Pathways) and 72 (1,000 Lives). Now invite players to invent their own video games and bring them to life. Have players work in teams of four or five.

Teams should consider the following in planning their games:

1. What is the game about?

2. What is the title of the game?

3. What characters appear in the game?

4. How do the characters move? What sounds do they make? Are they all as smart as each other? Are there heroes and villains?

5. Which sounds belong to which characters? What emotions do these sounds reflect?

6. What kinds of spaces are there in the story—places where they live, work, explore, fight, and so on?

7. What sort of pathways and patterns do the characters move in? What obstacles do they encounter?

8. What special powers are reserved for each of the characters?

9. Is there a way to win the game? Which character(s) will win and which will lose?

Have teams practice portraying their characters and moving along the pathways they have devised, reacting to obstacles and other characters along the way. When the games are ready, have teams perform them for the rest of the group.

Game Projects

In game projects, players work with the same material over the course of several class sessions. This gives players the opportunity to explore the material more deeply and bring out multiple facets. These projects will result in a piece that is ready for performance in front of an audience.

The first five games in this section (games 74 to 78) form a series. All are played with sets of index cards that must be prepared in advance. Each set of index cards provides players with a different element to include in their scene: character, location, time, and emotion. The series allows players to work with scenes of increasing complexity. In the remaining games, players write and act out their own productions based on various genres, many selected from the performance traditions of different cultures. These games give players the opportunity to learn about and appreciate the rich diversity of world drama.

74

Characters

Props: character cards (see below)

In advance, prepare a set of cards with the names of various personalities and professions. You might have players help brainstorm the characters: They could write down one personality or profession every day for a week. For example: movie star, executive, postal worker, construction worker, waiter, hacker, hairdresser, fortune teller, minister, Santa's elf, farmer, scientist, Olympic skater, escaped prisoner, mayor, bank robber, hot-dog vendor, rock musician, lifeguard.

Ask a player to pick a card and then walk forward a few steps, impersonating the character he has picked. You could choose one particular personality for every day of the week and work on that for 5 to 10 minutes with one or more players.

You can play this game any number of times. After players have practiced the simple portrayal of characters, make the game a little more complicated. Now when a player picks a character, she portrays that character in a typical situation. The player should perform actions that are specific to the character or profession: The scientist might perform lab experiments, peer through a microscope, take notes, and so on. What does each character experience in life? What kinds of things does he do?

Note: You can also use photos clipped from newspapers or magazines to suggest more character types.

Locations

Props: location cards (see below)

In advance, prepare a set of cards with the names of various locations. For example: North Pole, mall, airport, zoo, factory, library, volcano crater, convenience store, park, restaurant, desert island, courtroom, office, basketball court, Sahara Desert, subway car, beach, Mount Everest, emergency room, jail, health club, arcade, minefield.

Divide the group into teams of five or six players. Invite each team to pick a card and to create through its actions a sense of that location for the group. If people work in that location, some team members might portray those people in their professional roles. Others might portray customers, tourists, and so on—whatever characters might frequent that location. Teams shouldn't worry about acting out a story; they should simply make it clear to the audience where the scene takes place.

Help players to examine each location more deeply and see all the different possibilities it offers. Every location has something special about it. Some locations can be made "visible" by one person performing a single act, but there are also many locations where a number of things are happening at the same time. Encourage players to go beyond the most obvious actions.

Example: In a library, people read books. But a library offers many other possibilities: People might look for books on the shelves, use computers and copy machines, read stories to children, carry huge stacks of books around, and so on. The best way to show an audience that this is a library might be for one patron to raise a ruckus and be shushed by a librarian.

Have teams practice creating a series of locations as the group tries to guess each one.

Variation: With groups of young children, you may want to limit the number of location cards you make. For each location card, create a separate set of cards associated with that location. For example, to accompany the train station card, you might create a set of cards including: train, platform, bench, waiting room, ticket machine, newspaper stand, snack bar, and so on. Have teams choose a location card, and then choose four or five cards from the accompanying series. The team must include in their scene the features they chose.

76

Characters
and Locations

Props: character cards (see game 74), location cards (see game 75)

Acting really becomes fun when you know what your role entails, when you feel you really know what you're doing. In this game, players know both who and where they are. Invite teams of players to pick one card from the characters series and one from the locations series. Make sure players pick cards at random: The game works best when the people have nothing to do with the location. The team has to decide why they are there and what they are doing. The only rules are that they have to act together, stay in character, and do things that are associated with their job or character description. The players must see what is possible in this location, within the scope of their particular characters.

Example: Five railway workers find themselves at the North Pole. Perhaps they test the ice to see if it is strong enough to carry tracks and a train, then begin laying down tracks. What will happen when the train arrives?

Variation: Choose the characters and locations yourself, deliberately making them as incongruous as possible. You can think of the silliest combinations of people and places. A bunch of real estate agents find themselves in a house of mirrors? A group of burglars in a sauna? Plumbers in the zoo?

Time

Props: time cards (see below); character cards (see game 74); location cards (see game 75)

Game 76 (Characters and Locations) explored the *who* and *where* of a scene. Now we add another element: *When* does it happen? The time at which a scene takes place can have a huge influence on how it turns out. It becomes even more interesting to play a group of burglars in a sauna if the scene is set during the afternoon rush, when the sauna is filled with people. Remember, burglars are burglars wherever they are: They will still try to exercise their "art."

In advance, prepare a set of cards with different times—these could be times of day, dates, historical eras, or any other time you can think of. For example: dawn, lunchtime, rush hour, happy hour, 3:00 A.M., dinnertime, bedtime, prehistory, the nineteenth century, the Middle Ages, 500 years in the future, midnight on New Year's Eve, July Fourth, Thanksgiving, April 15 (tax day).

Divide the group into teams and have each team pick a character card, a location card, and a time card. Teams should make sure to include all these elements in their scenes. After about 20 minutes of practice, invite teams to perform their scenes for the group. Encourage players to remain in their roles, help them see the possibilities in the location, and remind them of the time of day.

Variation: Instead of having teams pick time cards at random, choose the ideal time for each scene yourself. Consider the characters and the location, and pick the time setting that will make for the most compelling drama. A scene with janitors in a minefield becomes even more exciting if it is set at night, in pitch darkness. Perhaps they use their mops and brooms to test where it is safe to go—and of course they leave the minefield spotless behind them. Do they all make it through?

Feelings

Props: emotion cards (see below); character cards (see game 74); location cards (see game 75); time cards (see game 77)

This game adds yet another element to the mosaic of game projects. Once the group has worked with characters, locations, and times (see games 74 through 77), it is time to combine all these with feelings. The burglars who ended up in the sauna during the afternoon rush have an overwhelming feeling about whatever conditions played a part in bringing them there. Perhaps they were annoyed or disappointed.

In advance, prepare a set of cards with different emotions, such as gleeful, furious, nostalgic, vain, depressed, flirtatious, zany, shy, suspicious, mischievous, fearful, tender, brokenhearted, argumentative, homesick, jaded, confused, jealous, excited, lonely.

Discuss with players how the element of emotion could affect a scene. How might characters display or express various emotions? Split the group into teams. Ask each team to choose a character card, a location card, a time card, and an emotion card. Then have each group take about 20 minutes to rehearse its scenario before performing it in front of the whole group. How do the scenes turn out?

This drama game is good for hours of fun!

Soap Opera

Props: a video camera and monitor (if possible); camera for still photos; bulletin board; tacks; masking tape; costumes; props

A soap opera is an exaggerated version of everyday life. Viewers identify with the characters and see their own dilemmas and relationships played out larger-than-life before them. Soaps hold viewers' interest with their numerous interlocking story lines, none of which is ever fully resolved. In this sense, soap operas are more realistic than most other forms of storytelling: As in life, there is never a tidy conclusion. In a soap, you are always left hanging with the questions "What's going to happen to...? Will he make it?" Tune in tomorrow!

Invite the group to create its own soap opera. Perhaps it could become an ongoing project: Players could perform an episode in the last 15 minutes of every class session or once a week. At one school, I supervised a soap that lasted an entire year, with an episode at the same time every week. The students came in eating their sandwiches, watched the latest episode, then left again. It was a kind of lunchtime theater. Each week the audience grew!

A project of this kind needs to be built in a series of steps:

- Encourage the group to develop a variety of characters and to plan out relationships between the characters: There should be friends, spouses, lovers, parents, children, allies, enemies, and so on.

- Ask each player to develop a character biography. A player should take notes on everything there is to know about her character: What is her personality? What happened in her past? How does she act under pressure? What relationships has she had? Does she have many friends? Does she have criminal tendencies? What does she have to hide? What are her ambitions?

- Guide players in making up a variety of story lines that include conflicts between characters. How will these conflicts develop? How might they be resolved?

- Have the group consider what locations the story lines will require and what props they will need to suggest these locations.

Players can use a large bulletin board to help them plan the story lines. Have players dress up as their characters, and take photo-

graphs. Tack photos of all the characters along the top of the board, creating a column for each character. Use lines of masking tape to create a grid on the board, with characters running along the top and scenes running down the left side. For each scene, players can find the boxes for the characters involved and tack notes with pieces of dialog or instructions about what is happening to that character at that point in the action. This way they can see each character's fate unroll as the story progresses. Once they have planned enough material for several episodes, players can write a few opening dialogs and begin rehearsals.

Before each performance there needs to be a rehearsal so that everyone knows the latest developments.

An episode might last about 15 minutes. Each episode begins with the theme song (you can use an existing tune). Then comes a 1-minute summary of the previous episode. This can be done in a series of tableaux—players freeze in poses representing each scene, then summarize the action in a few sentences. After this, players act out the new episode. Finally, players briefly preview the next episode in another series of tableaux and the theme song concludes the action for the day.

If players are able to produce a series of soap opera episodes, try to arrange for videotaping. Players might enjoy watching the whole series afterwards. Don't screen episodes until the whole serial is complete—particularly if the players do not have much experience with the medium of video. Many players are put off by watching themselves on video for the first time. People tend to have a different idea of themselves from what they see on screen. In any case, video-tape is not essential: Performing a new episode live every week is quite exciting enough!

Ancient Greek Drama

Props: research materials on ancient Greece; art materials for making masks (construction paper, cardboard, or papier-mâché); scissors; paints or markers for decorating masks

Have players research the dramatic traditions of ancient Greece. Depending on the group's proficiency and the time available, you might even have players read part or all of a Greek play in translation, such as *The Trojan Women* by Euripides. Invite players to create their own dramas inspired by those of ancient Greece. Players could choose a story from Greek myth or make up their own story. Give the group two or more sessions to do research, decide on a plot, and write a script together. Remind players that classical Greek dramas included a chorus that would say speeches in unison that commented on the action. Encourage them to include a chorus in their script. If the group wants a real challenge, it could write the script in verse form, with a regular pattern of rhythm and rhyme.

The next few sessions will be devoted to rehearsing the play and making masks, since ancient Greek actors all wore masks. Players should make several masks for each character in the play, showing different emotions. If a character is walking along happily and suddenly receives bad news, that player will need to remove her happy-face mask and replace it with a sorrowful one. Point out that the audience will not be able to see the actors' faces. Players must use their voices to make their characters come alive. When the "Greek drama" is ready, have the group perform it for an audience.

African Storytelling

Props: research materials on the African storytelling tradition; perhaps drums or other objects for making sound effects (optional)

This theater project is designed for players working individually. Have each player research storytelling traditions of Africa and the African diaspora (Caribbean; African American, including Gullah; and so on). The players should read stories, but they would benefit even more from listening to recordings (audio or videotape) of storytellers practicing their art. Players could make up their own stories to tell or choose existing stories to adapt. If players choose existing stories, encourage them to make the stories their own through revision, rephrasing, characterization, and so on. Try to avoid having players memorize existing stories word for word. Each player should develop one or more stories to present.

Encourage players to make their storytelling as lively and vivid as possible. Point out that storytellers often impersonate characters, speaking in different voices for each and perhaps acting out some of the action with simple movements. Storytellers also use call-and-response to involve the audience in the telling. They might teach the audience a short refrain to chant on cue at the appropriate moments in the story. Players could even make sound effects using drums or other objects. Players may want to rehearse their stories aloud in front of a mirror or try them out on family members. When players are ready, have them tell their stories to the group.

Southeast Asian Shadow Puppetry

Props: research materials on shadow puppetry; art materials for making shadow puppets (construction paper; scissors; wooden sticks, such as chopsticks; tape; paper fasteners; string; and so on); a white sheet and materials to hang it in order to form a screen; a bright, ad-justable lamp for lighting a screen

In shadow puppetry, puppets are placed between a light source and a translucent screen, so that only their shadows show. This art form is an important tradition in many Southeast Asian countries. Even today, audiences in Indonesia sit up late into the night, riveted by shadow puppet performances.

Invite players to create their own shadow puppet shows. Have players work in teams to research traditional shadow puppet designs, construction methods, and performance styles. Ask them to try making a few simple shadow puppets. Set up a shadow screen, using a white sheet with a bright light behind it. Then turn off the lights in the room and let the players experiment with shadow puppetry. What effects can players create by moving the puppets closer to and farther away from the screen?

Now have team members work together to develop a shadow play. Encourage them to think about what kinds of stories might work best in this medium. The play of shadows and light lends magic and mystery to a performance. Players might consider writing plays that involve characters who grow bigger or smaller, for instance, as they can create this effect by varying the puppet's distance from the screen. Once the plot of their shadow play has been decided, have them create the puppets to act it out. Depending on their proficiency, players might create simple, one-piece puppets, or complicated puppets with joints. Give teams time to rehearse their plays with the puppets and screen, and then have them perform for the group.

83

small
groups

Commedia
dell'arte

Props: research materials on commedia dell'arte; art materials for making masks (construction paper, cardboard, or papier-mâché); scissors; paints or markers for decorating masks; old clothing and fabric scraps for making simple costumes

The commedia dell'arte was a form of improvised and very physical comedy that originated in Renaissance Italy and influenced the performing arts all over Europe. "Slapstick comedy" is named after the noisemakers some commedia dell'arte players carried. Commedia dell'arte performers always played the same stock characters in every show. The most famous commedia dell'arte character is Arlecchino (Harlequin), the crafty and acrobatic trickster dressed in colorful patches. Many of these characters were represented by specific masks, often with exaggerated features. The actors agreed on the skeleton of a plot before performing, but never used written scripts: All dialog was improvised on stage.

Ask teams of players to research commedia dell'arte characters and plots. Then have each team member choose a stock commedia dell'arte character to develop. Depending on the time available, players might create masks and costumes to represent their characters. Each player should research the characteristics, style of movement, and behavior typical of his character. Then have the team work together to come up with a slapstick comedy scenario involving all the characters they have chosen. As in commedia dell'arte, ask players to work out only the skeleton of the plot and leave all dialog to be improvised. When teams are ready, have them perform for the group.

Pacific Northwest Transformation Masks

Props: research materials on Pacific Northwest Native Americans; art materials for making masks (construction paper, cardboard, or papier-mâché); scissors; paints or markers for decorating masks

Native Americans of the Pacific Northwest have a long—and continuing—tradition of masterful mask making. Some Pacific Northwest masks are highly stylized, with bold abstract designs. Others are vivid and realistic portraits of people. Transformation masks are the most elaborate and fascinating. The outer face of a transformation mask opens to reveal a second, and sometimes a third, face underneath. These masks are used to act out complex stories about spirits, the workings of the universe, and a particular group's heritage.

Have teams of players research Native American tribes of the Pacific Northwest and the tradition of transformation masks. Then team members should create an idea for a play involving transformations: perhaps from human to animal or (for a modern twist) human to robot. Players could adapt stories from Pacific Northwest tribes or make up their own stories. Before each team works out all the details for the play and writes a script, have the team members create the masks they will need. Transformation masks are difficult to make, and players may need to adjust their plans. Players may find, for instance, that it is easier to transform a bird into a human than it is to turn a human into a bird—it is hard to conceal a long beak under a relatively flat human face. If creating hinged masks that open up proves too complicated, players could create masks that fit over each other. This way, they could simply remove one mask to reveal another. After they finish the masks, have teams fully develop their play ideas and rehearse with the masks. Then invite teams to perform for the group.

85

Shakespearean Monologues

Props: annotated copies of Shakespearean plays

Shakespeare is the most widely revered playwright in the English language. Many students find Shakespeare's plays daunting because of the language, which is often in verse and archaic in vocabulary and syntax. This project gives advanced players the chance to study an example of Shakespearean language carefully, use notes to decipher its nuances and references, and make it their own through performance.

Unless players are very familiar with Shakespeare, suggest specific monologues for them to develop. The project might be more interesting if you avoid the most famous monologues ("To be or not to be..." and so on) and suggest speeches that are lighter in tone or that will strike a chord for teenagers. A few possibilities are Viola's long speech in Act II, scene ii of *Twelfth Night,* Orlando's opening speech in Act I, scene i of *As You Like It,* Benedick's speech at the beginning of Act II, scene iii of *Much Ado About Nothing,* and Juliet's speech at the very end of Act IV, scene iii of *Romeo and Juliet.*

Have players read the speeches in an annotated student's edition of the plays. In the annotated edition, players will find summaries of the play and of each scene, as well as notes explaining archaic language and references. Have players use the summaries to learn the plot of the play well enough to explain their character's situation to an audience. Ask players to study their chosen speeches until they understand what the character is saying and feeling. Then have them develop dramatic readings of the speeches, using tone of voice, tempo, and so on to convey meaning and emotion. Depending on their proficiency and the time available, you might have players memorize the monologues. After a few sessions of study and practice, have each player get up in front of the group, explain her character's situation at the time of the monologue, and read (or recite) the speech aloud.

Latino Folk Theater

Props: research materials on traditional Latino pageants and performances; old clothing and cloth scraps for making costumes

Have the group research the Spanish-influenced folk theater of the Americas, including such performances and pageants as *Los Pastores* ("The Shepherds' Play") and *Moros y Cristianos* ("The Moors and the Christians"). These performances were introduced to the region by Spanish missionaries in the effort to convert Native Americans to Christianity, but they have taken on a uniquely New World flavor. The plays are not exclusively religious in tone: *Moros y Christianos* dramatizes exciting battles on horseback between Spanish and Muslim fighters. *Los Pastores* includes many humorous episodes as it tells the story of the devil's attempts to waylay shepherds journeying to visit the baby Jesus. In both of these examples, one group of characters is portrayed as evil (the devils and the Moors). Both performances involve a conflict between good and evil, in which good inevitably prevails.

After players have read some descriptions of these traditional performances, invite them to work as a group to make up colorful pageants of their own in which good and evil do battle. Players might find recordings of songs in Spanish that form part of the performance of *Los Pastores* and other plays—if players are proficient in Spanish, perhaps they can work some of these songs into the storyline of their pageant. When the pageant is ready, have the group perform it for an audience.

Bollywood Movies

Props: Hindi films on video; CD or cassette player and recordings of popular (American) songs; video camera with tripod

More feature films are produced each year in Mumbai, India (formerly known as Bombay) than in any other city—including Hollywood. That's how Bombay got the nickname "Bollywood." Find some hit Indian movies (subtitled in English) online or at a local shop that sells Indian clothing and products. You might show brief excerpts in class, but let players checkout the videos to watch at home: Indian movies often last three hours or more. Discuss the typical features of a Hindi film: These movies are romances, musicals, action-adventure thrillers, and comedies all in one. Hindi films tend to center on troubled romance, include several song-and-dance numbers, have sprawling plots that stretch over long periods of time and involve lots of characters, and throw some exciting action in for good measure.

Invite players to make up and star in their own Bollywood-style film. Have them develop a plot expansive enough for every player to play a significant character. Suggest that players choose some popular (American) songs with lyrics that fit situations in their plot. Players can insert the songs into the script, work out choreography, and practice dancing and lip synching to recordings of the songs. When players have developed and practiced their movie, have them perform it and film it with a video camera.

Status Games

Status is a person's standing in a group. In different contexts, status might mean popularity, social class, or rank (general versus foot soldier; executive versus secretary). People with high status may be arrogant, feel self-important, and look down on others. People with low status may follow orders, defer to others, and feel like the underdog. Of course, status is not set in stone: A person's status may be different in different groups, a person's status can change over time, and a person's official rank or class may not reflect the realities of his or her true influence.

This series of drama games explores status. It is the last section in the book and also the most difficult. These games are designed for older players in middle school and high school. You will need to practice the games yourself before introducing them to a class—they cannot be played without some preparation.

Two Strangers

Tell players that in this game, everyone will play the same scene: Two strangers meet on a park bench. Divide the group into pairs. Explain that in the scene, one partner feels very important because of his profession, while the other has no job and feels inferior. In this game the status is not challenged, so if a player begins the game in the superior role, that's how she ends it. After playing the game once, partners should switch roles and play it again. Afterwards, have the group discuss their reactions to playing the two roles.

Example: While out walking his dog, a company director meets an unemployed person. The director feels very superior, while the unemployed person feels like a loser. Will the director help the unemployed person or not? Is there any solution to the problem in the sketch?

Two Sentences

Props: cards with opening sentences (see below)

In advance, make up several scenarios involving two characters, one of low status and the other of high status. For each scenario, create two cards, each with one character's opening line of dialog.

Example:

Card 1: Sorry I'm late! I promise to come in early tomorrow.

Card 2: How could you be late on a day like today? I'm pretty close to firing you right now.

Have pairs of players take turns coming to the front. Hand each partner a card. They should not discuss the cards with each other. Now have them read the lines of dialog on their cards and improvise the remainder of the scene for the group. Based on the opening lines, partners must decide whether their characters have low or high status and then act out the scene accordingly. (In the example above, the player with card 1 is obviously the one with low status.) Do partners assume the right status levels?

small
groups

Losers

In games 88 (Two Strangers) and 89 (Two Sentences), players portrayed characters of high and low status. Explain that in this game, all the characters have low status. (In this game, we explore low status in terms of self-esteem rather than social class: The characters feel themselves to be losers.) Invite two volunteers to help you demonstrate the game. Tell the volunteers that the action takes place in the laundromat. The characters come into the laundromat with a big load of wash. Neither of them knows how to work the machines. They can't figure it out—they're both completely hopeless. They don't blame each other or try to outdo each other. Call on a third volunteer to join the game: She's another loser. All three play out their helplessness until you stop the scene.

Now ask teams of about four players to make up sketches featuring low status. The characters all feel themselves to be equal, so they don't try to put each other down or to ingratiate themselves to each other. Do they remain a collection of losers (as in the example), or become a gang of comrades who work together well? It is interesting to see how the players make a study of the equal status in the game. This is a difficult assignment!

Topsy-Turvy

In Renaissance Europe—a society in which social status was very rigid—many communities had one day each year on which the lords served the servants, and the whole class system was temporarily turned upside-down. People have expectations of how a high-status person behaves and how a person with low status behaves. When someone goes against these expectations, it can be humorous—and thought provoking.

Tell players that this game, like games 88 (Two Strangers) and 89 (Two Sentences), involves a scene with two characters—one has a high status and the other a low status. Explain that this game is different because the person with low status acts as if his status were high, and vice versa. Have players sit in a semicircle around an open space for performing. Invite two volunteers to demonstrate the game by acting out a scene you will describe to them.

Example: A great lord is getting dressed for a party, and his servant is helping him. But instead of lording it over the servant, the lord is constantly asking the servant's advice about dress, how to act at the party, and so on. It becomes clear that the servant is running his "master's" life.

Now have new pairs of players come to the front to act scenes along similar lines. Decide beforehand which player has high status and which has low status, but have players improvise the scenes without further planning.

small groups

Reversal of Fortune

Social status in a group (popularity) can shift quickly. Success on the football field or hosting a great party can boost someone to popularity, while being caught in a lie might make someone unpopular. Some people put others down to try to boost their own social status. Like games 88, 89, and 91, this game begins with characters of high and low status. This time, in the course of the scene the characters switch status. One character grows in status because the other moves downwards.

Divide the group into teams of four or five. Each team should choose one player to begin the scene with high status and another player to begin with low status. The others will take on the role of the group and show with their behavior what status the two main characters have. To demonstrate the game, you might ask one team to act out the following:

Example: Students are waiting in a classroom for test results to be handed back. One nerd worries about her grade, and a popular guy takes the opportunity to put her down, calling her stupid. The others follow along and mock her. Then the papers are handed back, and it turns out the nerd did well, while the popular guy failed. The nerd turns the tables, teasing the guy and telling him to worry about his own grades instead of making fun of others. The group admires her courage, and the nerd's status rises while the popular guy's status goes down.

Have other teams act out other scenes along similar lines. Encourage players to lead up to the change in status slowly, rather than switching a character's status instantaneously. This makes the scene more interesting.

The Audience Speaks

Props: strips of paper with dialog written on them (see below)

The audience is an important player in this status game. As a scene is acted out, the audience has the power to raise or lower a character's status and propel the action in a different direction.

In advance, write single lines of dialog on strips of paper.

Examples:

- I don't believe it! I picked the winning lottery ticket!

- I have to tell you that my best friend is a pig.

- And that's why I wrote this song. I'll sing it to you.

- I know all about your little secret.

- I've done it all wrong. Can you forgive me?

Call four or five players to come to the front. They will act out an improvisational scene, while the other players are the audience. Pass out dialog strips to all the audience members. Explain that audience members should silently read their strips and watch the scene carefully. Each audience member should picture what would happen if a character recited the words written on his slip of paper. If an audience member sees an opportunity to use his words to change a character's status, he should raise his hand. You will interrupt the scene periodically and call on an audience member. The audience member should hand his slip of paper to the player he has chosen. The scene begins again, and that player must incorporate the line of dialog as soon as possible. The words will have repercussions for that player's character: They will raise or lower her status.

The players at the front should decide whether their characters have high or low status and then begin their scene. The subject for the scene can be borrowed from another game, such as game 54 (The Waiting Room) or game 55 (The Party). Every few minutes, interrupt the scene and give an audience member the chance to intervene. Don't stop the scene too often: Too many interruptions will upset the progress of the story.

Rags to Riches

Status is not permanent. People with low status dream of one day achieving a high status, and many make their dreams come true. Newspapers, novels, television shows, and movies are filled with Cinderella stories and self-made millionaires.

Invite teams of players to make up and perform skits that trace a character from a low status to a high status. This might mean a rags-to-riches story, the story of the making of a star, or the story of a leader's rise to greatness. Have teams either write a script or work out the plot and improvise the dialog during performance. Teams should make up and develop the skits in the first session. In the second session, give teams some time for practice and then invite them to perform for the group.

Tragedy

A tragic figure falls from greatness: Tragedy traces a path from high status to low status. High school students are usually required to read tragedies, so many players will be familiar with Shakespearean tragic figures, such as Hamlet, Macbeth, and Othello. They may also know of historical figures who fell from high status, such as Napoleon and Joan of Arc.

Divide the group into teams and have them develop skits that follow the tragic model. Players might choose tragic situations from everyday life, such as a sports hero who loses confidence and begins losing games. Teams should be sure their skits center on a tragic figure: A character who falls from a high status to a low status. Teams can work together to write a script, or they can work out the general events of the plot and improvise the dialog during perform-ance. Give teams one session to make up and develop their skits. In the next session, teams can practice and then present their skits to the group.

Comedy

Props: videos of the Three Stooges, the Marx Brothers, and other comedians (optional)

Comedy is all about status. The art of comedy involves puncturing inflated egos and expectations. In order to make jokes, the comedian may lower his own status (self-deprecating humor) or that of others (insult comedy, parody, satire). Slapstick comedies are full of funny status games. The Three Stooges, for instance, are always putting each other down and trying to outdo each other, even though all three are idiots. Comedians often make fools of themselves or others.

If possible, show the group video clips of some slapstick comedians, such as the Three Stooges, and discuss the role of status in comedy. Divide the group into teams of about four players. Have teams choose comic characters or develop some of their own. Then give them an hour or more to prepare a comic sketch involving putdowns and other status changes. Finally, have teams perform their skits for the group.

Sunglasses

Props: a pair of sunglasses for each player

Movie stars wear sunglasses so their fans won't recognize them, but the glasses make them look even more glamorous. Sunglasses make secret service agents and highway patrol officers even more intimidating. Anybody looks cooler in a good pair of sunglasses.

In advance, ask each player to bring in a pair of sunglasses. Have players mill around the room without their glasses, briefly greeting everyone they meet. Now have everyone put on sunglasses and repeat the exercise. After a few minutes, get the group to talk about whether they felt different with their glasses on. Many people find that wearing sunglasses alters their status.

Divide the group into teams of about four and invite each team to make up a sketch involving sunglasses and status. Encourage teams to include some characters who wear glasses and some who do not. After 20 minutes of preparation, have teams perform their sketches for the group.

98

The Wrong Room

Everyone knows what it's like to go into the wrong room. It's mortifying to burst into a living room where a tense conversation is going on; an office you weren't allowed to go into; the teachers' lounge at school; even the wrong classroom, if everyone looks up at you expectantly.

Have the group sit in a semicircle. Call on players to stand up one by one and mime going through a door into some imaginary wrong room. They can also say appropriate words—apologies, excuses, and so on. Encourage players to make their words and actions as realistic as possible.

The first time the game is played, you can use the most obvious situations, such as the teachers' lounge. After this introduction, the next players can each think of a new kind of room to enter. How can players raise or lower their status through their reaction to finding themselves in the wrong room? Can they think up a scenario in which entering the wrong room turns out to be lucky? Prompt less-experienced players by acting the part of a person in the room, asking intruders, "What are you doing in here?" and so on.

The **Letter**

Props: several fictional letters (see below); a table and two chairs

A love letter, a final demand, a college rejection notice, an envelope full of money.... The daily mail can bring success or failure, joy or sorrow, good news or bad.

In advance, write some fictional letters that would have a significant effect on the recipient. You might use some of the examples above, or perhaps write a job offer, a ransom note, a report card, a draft notice, and so on.

To begin the game, place a letter on the table. Invite a player to come up, discover the letter, and read it. The letter is not addressed to this player; he reads it without permission. While the letter is being read, or perhaps just afterward, invite another player to come up and act the part of the letter's proper recipient. Does the recipient catch the other player in the act of reading the letter and become angry? Does the knowledge of the letter's contents give the other player power over the recipient? Have the two players act out the scene and develop the changes in status caused by the letter. Place a new letter on the table and invite two different players to act out another scene.

Variation: Instead of a letter, place an object on the table and invite one player to "borrow" the object and either break or lose it. The second player to enter is the owner of the object.

The **Boss**

The business world is one place in our society where status is clearly demarcated. Everyone knows who is boss. In this game, players portray a business hierarchy. Guide volunteers in acting out a few examples in different types of organizations: The boss gives her employee an assignment, a message, or something of the kind. The employee passes the job on to the person below him in rank, and this person does the same.... Thus you can reveal the chain of command in an organization. The differences in rank must come across clearly.

Divide the group into teams and have each team make up a sketch about a business hierarchy. Encourage the team members to work out the details of the differences in rank. After 20 minutes, the teams can perform their sketches for the others. Encourage players to behave professionally: Make sure they don't simply berate their inferiors. Are the higher-ups encouraging? patronizing? manipulative? In what subtle ways do status differences show themselves?

Hero and Sidekick

Batman and Robin, Don Quixote and Sancho Panza, Xena and Gabrielle: Literature and popular culture are filled with heroes and sidekicks. Players may be familiar with heroes and sidekicks from animated movies such as *Shrek*, *Mulan*, and *Monsters, Inc.*

Invite pairs of players to make up sketches about heroes and sidekicks. Have them develop two scenes. In the first, the dynamic duo have an ordinary adventure in which their roles are never called into question: The sidekick almost makes a fatal mistake, the hero saves the sidekick, and so on. The second scene makes their relationship more complicated: Perhaps the sidekick questions a moral judgment the hero has made, or the sidekick saves the day and begins to get ideas about becoming a hero in his own right. After 20 minutes of practice, invite pairs to perform their scenes for the group.

The Games Arranged According to Age Groups

Elementary School Children

(K-Grade 5)

1. Flattery Will Get You Everywhere
6. Follow the Feeling
13. The Gift
14. Exchange It
25. Glass Slippers and Giants' Boots

Older Children and Teens

(Grades 3-8)

3. Ready, Set, Alphabet!
27. Dress Each Other
82. Southeast Asian Shadow Puppetry

Older Children and Teens

(Grades 3-12)

8. Alice the Amiable Anteater
10. Solve the Problem!
11. I Want You to Give Me…
12. The Storyteller and the Actor
15. Spoil the Picture
16. From Bad to Worse
17. My Life as a Football
19. The Doorbell
20. Slow Motion
23. The Route
28. Time Warp
32. Through the Camera's Lens
34. The Mirror
37. Rewind
39. Forgotten Items
43. Body Tension

44. Out of Thin Air
45. Air and Balance
48. Invisible Object
49. Weightless
55. The Party
59. Moods
60. Two Moods
62. Babble
65. Word Game
69. Locomotion
70. Emotions and Sounds
71. Obstacles and Pathways
72. 1,000 Lives
73. Game Design
74. Characters
75. Locations
76. Characters and Locations
77. Time
78. Feelings
84. Pacific Northwest Transformation Masks
86. Latino Folk Theater

Teens in Middle School and High School

(Grades 6-12)

7. Worth 1,000 Words
18. Taking Over
30. In a Manner of Speaking
31. Out of Uniform
33. Back Talk
35. Who Is the Mirror?
36. Equality
41. Be Something
46. Spotters
47. Soloist and Group
51. Tug-of-War
52. Feel the Motion
54. The Waiting Room
56. The End

Teens in High School,
(Grades 9-12)

All Ages

More *SmartFun* Activity Books for ages 4 and up

The SmartFun activity books encourage imagination, social interaction, and self-expression in children. The series is widely used in homes, schools, day-care centers, clubs, and summer camps.

101 MUSIC GAMES FOR CHILDREN: Fun and Learning with Rhythm and Song *by* Jerry Storms

All you need to play these 101 music games are music tapes or CDs and simple instruments, many of which kids can have fun making from common household items.

101 MORE MUSIC GAMES FOR CHILDREN: New Fun and Learning with Rhythm and Song *by* Jerry Storms

This action-packed compendium offers ingenious song and dance activities from a variety of cultures. These help children enjoy themselves and develope a love for music.

101 DANCE GAMES FOR CHILDREN: Fun and Creativity with Movement *by* Paul Rooyackers

The games in this book combine movement and play in ways that encourage children to interact and express how they feel in creative fantasies and without words.

101 DRAMA GAMES FOR CHILDREN: Fun and Learning with Acting and Make-Believe *by* Paul Rooyackers

These include introduction games, sensory games, pantomime games, story games, sound games, games with masks, and games with costumes.

101 MOVEMENT GAMES FOR CHILDREN: Fun and Learning with Playful Moving *by* Huberta Wiertsema

These games include variations on old favorites such as "Duck, Duck, Goose" as well as new games such as "Mirroring," "Equal Pacing," and "Moving Joints."

UPCOMING BOOKS IN THIS SERIES...

101 MORE DANCE GAMES FOR CHILDREN: New Fun and Creativity with Movement *by* Paul Rooyackers   *November 2002*

Introductory Games, Animal Dance Games, Character Dance Games, Street Dance Games, Dance a Story, Dancing with Props, and Dance Notations.

YOGA GAMES FOR CHILDREN: Fun and Fitness with Postures, Movements and Breath *by* Danielle Bersma and Marjoke Visscher *December 2002*

A playful introduction to yoga for children ages 6–12. The games help young people develop body awareness, physical strength, and flexibility.

For more information visit www.hunterhouse.com